GREAT TRAIN ROBBERY CONFIDENTIAL

**THE COP AND
THE ROBBER
FOLLOW
NEW LINES
OF ENQUIRY**

GREAT TRAIN ROBBERY CONFIDENTIAL

THE COP AND THE ROBBER FOLLOW NEW LINES OF ENQUIRY

GRAHAM SATCHWELL

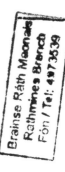

The History Press

Graham Satchwell served in every rank of CID within the British Transport Police (1978–99), for many years serving as Detective Superintendent, Britain's most senior railways detective. During his service he was awarded numerous commendations by crown court judges and chief constables among others. This is his second book for The History Press.

Cover credit: View from a footpath near Ledburn, Buckinghamshire over the West Coast Main Line, towards 'Sears Crossing' where robbers took control of a mail train during the Great Train Robbery, 8 August 1963. (Sealman via Wikimedia Commons, CC SA3.0)

First published 2019

The History Press
97 St George's Place, Cheltenham,
Gloucestershire, GL50 3QB
www.thehistorypress.co.uk

British Library Cataloguing in Publication Data.
A catalogue record for this book is available from the British Library.

ISBN 978 0 7509 9232 9

Typesetting and origination by The History Press
Printed and bound in Great Britain by TJ International Ltd.

CONTENTS

FOREWORD

BY LORD MACKENZIE OF FRAMWELLGATE OBE LLB [HONS]

This is the third occasion on which I have written a foreword for a book by Graham. The first book was significant and led to his giving expert evidence to the United States' Senate. The subject was counterfeit medicines and organised crime. That book exposed that vile international trade like no other had done before.

The second book was a memoir, which *The Guardian* described as 'the best of the genre'.

This book is about the Great Train Robbery, which I have reason to remember well, as it occurred within only months of me joining the police service in 1963. It has the shared strength of both of its predecessors; it is conversational in style, amusing in parts and easy reading.

But this book also has the individual strengths of both aforementioned: it exposes Graham's skills and drive as a very experienced detective, to uncover the truth about serious crime, but in the context of the sort of criminality that he personally confronted for over thirty years.

It is a testament to Graham that a notorious gangster, who was put away by Graham in 1982, was willing to work with him to find a way to tell the truth written here.

It is no surprise to me therefore that the book really does shed new light on the Great Train Robbery, as well as to correct an injustice perpetuated against an innocent man. Even though this crime occurred over fifty years ago, it displays the motivation, greed and destructiveness of criminality which is just as relevant today as it was in the swinging sixties. This book is a compelling read!

A NOTE FROM MARILYN WISBEY

I first met Graham Satchwell in 1981. I was about 27 years old at the time and my father had just been taken into custody for his part in handling some travellers' cheques that had been stolen from the Royal Mail.

My mum and I went to a building in Tavistock Place, Bloomsbury to visit Dad. I remember it well because the place was nothing like a police station. It felt like an old hospital.

We met Graham at the lift and he was pleasant and polite. I remember that Mum said how handsome he was for a detective. Funny the things you remember.

They let me and Mum see Dad. They seemed to have treated him alright. But of course it was really bad that he had been arrested again; it meant he could be recalled to prison for the Great Train Robbery. He could have got another heavy sentence for the travellers' cheques too.

Detective Inspector Satchwell, as he was then, objected to every bail application we made, and Dad stayed locked up for nearly two years awaiting trial. Dad never complained of course; he treated all that as par for the course.

I didn't meet Graham again until after Dad's stroke. Peter Kent, a friend to Dad going back many years, introduced Graham to me at the hospital. My dad and Graham had been writing a book together, not this one but a mix of fact and fiction, a novel. I've read the draft that my dad helped Graham with and it's realistic. Obviously, both of them working together, you would expect it to be about right. It's a good story too.

Graham visited Dad two or three times as his condition worsened. I remember once when Dad was fed up, Graham took him out in a wheelchair to give him a bit of fresh air and a change of scenery. Graham always treated Dad eye-to-eye, on equal terms. Dad was the same with everyone as well. That's the way it's supposed to be.

Graham has asked me an awful lot of questions over the last two years, many of which I didn't know the answer to. I have been asking myself many of those same questions over many years. The process of working with Graham has helped me understand more of what went on. That might seem strange, but Dad would never tell me or Mum any more than he had to. He kept his work to himself – that was the rule and he stuck to it. But of course very occasionally I saw things, heard things, met people, took phone calls. It would have been impossible for me to have been kept in the dark completely, even as a child.

There are some big questions that remain unanswered. I would have liked to get closure on them all, but that will never happen now. But I have learned more recently about the involvement of the Sansom family, and I've been able to share what I know about the Pembrokes, Billy Hill, and so on. That's been helpful to me.

And I've read the book that follows. I can't add much to it. I don't know any more than what's there, and half of that I could not personally swear to. But it all makes sense and Dad had no reason to mislead anyone, not at that stage in his life anyway. There is a lot of truth in this book that has not been revealed before.

The Great Train Robbery made Dad very rich for a short space of time and famous forever. But it completely shattered our family. I would not recommend a life of crime to anybody. A lot of young blokes like the glamour and the reputation that they think that sort of life will bring. And that way of life means you don't have to commit to working most days of your life.

You never have to set an alarm clock and if you've got your head screwed on, the money is good as well.

But most men and women want more than that. They want trusting, loving relationships, family and peace of mind.

I definitely do not recommend a life of crime.

ACKNOWLEDGEMENTS

First, I must acknowledge the help given by Tom Wisbey. There have been many sources for what follows, but undoubtedly the most significant was the train robber Tom Wisbey.

Before 2014, Tom Wisbey simply knew me as the former detective who led the case that resulted in his being re-imprisoned in 1981. In 2014, I discovered we had a mutual friend, a very discreet, elderly gentleman called Peter Kent. Peter arranged for Tom and me to meet and when we did, Tom readily agreed to help me with my Great Train Robbery book. He put himself out to help me and continued to do so for several months before the stroke that led to his death. I will say much more about Tom later, but it is certainly the case that without his input this book would be much less than it is.

After Tom's death, his daughter Marilyn was kind enough, for over two years, to help me make sense of some of the things that Tom had told me. I thank her for that.

I think I understand for the first time in my life why some books contain acknowledgements pages that provide a cast long enough to typify a Hollywood movie. I know now that some books really are thanks to the contribution of many. This is one of them.

The British Transport Police History Group, which is made up chiefly of retired BTP officers, was helpful in giving access to papers that they held and for appealing for information.

When this book was almost fully drafted I encouraged the participation of Channel 4 TV. They were extremely determined to check out my background. I put them in contact with two men that I worked with in the early 1980s: Martyn Leadbetter, a national figure in the world of fingerprint evidence, and former Detective Sergeant Peter Bennett (Met Police C11, NSY). Both men were keen to help, and both recalled important aspects of those days, some of which I had forgotten and which were important to the story.

Members of the same Channel 4 crew were determined to test my assertion that a certain handwritten note was written by Tom Wisbey. Obviously, I do not have access to forensic science these days, so I must thank Amanda Langley, fingerprint expert at the City of London Police for her great help and hospitality.

I know little of the rules of railway signalling and I am indebted to David Smith (formerly a high-ranking rail professional of many years' standing) for his insight and for sharing his considerable knowledge of the railways of the early 1960s.

Early in 2019, I wrote to the railways' staff pensioners' publication *Penfriend* and they kindly published an appeal for information about the robbery. The response was tremendous and a thank you is owed to the editor and all those fellow 'old folk' who took the time and trouble to get in touch.

Much of what they told me was of value, and all of it was very interesting. Leslie Watson from Cardiff became my instant expert on the realities of being a train driver in the early '60s. Tony Glazebrook helped me tremendously with a copy of the BR Internal Enquiry papers given to him a few years after the robbery. Nigel Adams (Luton Model Railway Club) and Geoffrey Higginbotham (former TPO worker) were both helpful and entertaining. Lindsey Bowen, Bill Faint, and Malread Harvey also deserve my thanks.

John Tidy joined the BTP at the same time as me but after a couple of years had the good sense to leave. A few years later a successful career in publishing led him to the USA. I'm pleased to say that he resettled in the London area relatively recently and helped a good deal with research for this book. Thank you, John.

Similarly, I was delighted to speak to several other old BTP colleagues including former PC Gordon Blake, who was on duty on the night of the Great Train Robbery and awaited its arrival at Euston station. Similarly, Stan Wade for his important contribution and with whom I worked as a young constable (more of him later) and Eddie Coppinger who also remembered 1963 and served in the British Army with one of the train robbers.

Peter 'Chippy' Woods, a very long-since retired detective inspector now living 'Up Norf', made contact with me for the first time in well over thirty years. He knew Buster Edwards and made the tea (as a young detective) for the CID bosses engaged in the investigation. More significantly, as part of the specialist mailbag squad of the time, he investigated some of those crimes committed by the South Coast Raiders.

Of course, there are others too: John Wyn-De-Bank, Peter and Stephen Kent, Colin Boyce from Thames Valley Police (who kindly allowed me to reproduce a couple of photographs) and Paul Bickley at NSY are chief amongst them.

Arwel Owen, son of the guard who was assaulted by the robbers six months before the Great Train Robbery, played a very important role in uncovering the truth. Several years ago, Arwel wrote an excellent book describing those events and when I approached him this year for the first time, he was extremely accommodating.

In later chapters you will see important photographic evidence, but without the staff of Bournemouth Newspapers that evidence would have been lost and so my thanks to them for their very necessary help.

But when it comes to moving from a draft book to a publication, things get really tough. Thank goodness for The History Press and editor Amy Rigg. Amy was so encouraging, consistent, positive and constructive; she could not have made the process easier.

PREFACE

The story of the Great Train Robbery (GTR) has surely been told, retold and embroidered as much as any crime in history. Anyone coming to the subject for the first time and reviewing the materials available would be left misled and confused. However, it is easy to point back to facts proven beyond question, facts readily accepted by all concerned, and where such evidence is not available, overwhelming logic. In addition to stripping back the mass and mess of misleading assertions to a coherent truth, I have discovered much that has not been revealed before.

The GTR took place in 1963. To fully understand the public response it is necessary to appreciate that different social norms operated. A firm and undisguised class structure was in place. Those who had real financial or political power had their own vocabulary and spoke naturally with, or affected, a particular accent. That accent was somewhere between that required of a BBC commentator and a member of the Royal Family. Such people dressed in a way that was exclusively theirs; they had foreign holidays, motorcars and particular leisure pursuits, went to university, and did particular jobs that were exclusively theirs. It was a fairly rigid class system in which everyone was 'supposed to know their place'.

Today of course, that world has been turned on its head. Politicians try to disguise their public-school accents, money rules no matter how it was gained, everyone has a 'motor', princes drink beer and foreign holidays are given to people 'on benefits'. But by 1963, the winds of change (to use a phrase of the time) were blowing gently but building. The 'common man' (and I was a very young one at the time) felt rebellious: 'Why should I be expected to show deference to people who just happen to have been born into money?' That societal change is only important in this context because it reflects the two different ways that the robbery, and the robbers, were viewed.

The basic facts are well known. On the night of 7/8 August 1963, a gang of about fifteen held up a mail train that was making a routine journey from Glasgow to London Euston. The train concerned was a mail train known as a 'travelling post office' (TPO). It had no passengers but about 100 postal workers. They busied themselves sorting the mail as the train sped through the night. The two lead coaches held about £2.6 million in banknotes of various denominations (being returned to the Bank of England for cleaning or destruction).

The TPO train made its usual scheduled stops (to pick up more mail), the last of which (before London) was Rugby. At Rugby, the train crew who had brought the train down from Scotland finished their duties. Driver Mills and Second Man Whitby replaced them. The train left Rugby on time but near a quiet spot called Ledburn in Buckinghamshire it was attacked.

The robbers stopped the train just south of Leighton Buzzard by altering two trackside railway signals. The driver had fully expected to have green lights all the way, but one of the robbers, Roger Cordrey, was highly skilled. With an accomplice, he ensured a trackside signal was changed to yellow (or amber), indicating 'caution'. This would cause the driver to slow right down and prepare to stop. The second false signal was red, and Driver Mills immediately brought the train to a stop at the signals at Sears Crossing.

As soon as the train stopped the robbers busied themselves disconnecting the locomotive and front two coaches from the remainder. They overpowered the driver and his assistant (Second Man) and divided the locomotive and two 'lead' coaches from the rest of the train. Having separated the train into two, the robbers forced the train driver to move the locomotive and two coaches forward to Bridego Bridge. There the gang smashed their way into the coaches and set upon and subdued the postmen working within.

The robbers unloaded about 100 mailbags from the train and made off with over £2.6 million in untraceable used banknotes. Only just over £400,000 was ever recovered or accounted for. The whereabouts of the rest has remained a mystery.

It is generally believed that three of the robbers who attended the train that night were never caught. It was by far the biggest robbery ever committed in Britain. The Establishment expressed indignity, outrage and a determination to punish. Following the trial at Aylesbury, sentences of up to thirty years were imposed. Those sentences were immense; they were double the length that one would expect to receive if convicted of committing an armed robbery and discharging firearms. Any policeman or lawyer at the time might have anticipated a sentence of perhaps ten to fourteen years. The response to those sentences was largely twofold. The Establishment, as you will see later, was determined to bolster the case against the accused, and after the sentences were meted out, equally keen to justify them. Conversely, many of the general public began a sort of celebration of the robbers who it seemed had stolen from those that could afford it using minimum force. For many it seemed as if Robin Hood and his Merry Men lived again.

Certain members of the Establishment went overboard in their determination to punish and vilify. Records of events after sentencing are remarkable, as you will see later, in the stories told by those in authority about the threat that such a major crime held against society in general. This of course merely painted establishment figures even more vividly as part of the 'Sheriff of Nottingham's gang'. You will see how these two very different interpretations of events have coloured both the evidence at the trial and what has been written and said since.

No one has ever stood trial for being the organiser, and no one has ever stood trial accused of supplying the very necessary inside information. From the earliest days after the robbery, there have been all sorts of outlandish accounts of who the missing robbers might have been. There have been even more ludicrous stories 'revealing' who orchestrated it all. The creation and dissemination of all that guff has been caused by an undeserved (and unpaid for) desire by shallow individuals seeking fame and infamy. In addition some professional writers and broadcasters have seemed keen to get a story at almost any cost to their own integrity and greater cost to the innocent. Then there were the robbers themselves, determined to make a buck and to add to the number of individuals keen to buy them a drink or a meal.

If you read any reasonable selection of books about the robbery, you will soon discover that certain key facts have remained open to speculation. These include:

- Was there a mastermind?
- Who was the key insider who gave the vital information to the robbers?
- Who were the robbers that got away?

This book sheds new light on those key areas, not by empty speculation but by evidence and logic. In doing so, it debunks some of the nonsense that has been commonly believed, for instance that Bruce Reynolds was the leader of the gang, that the robbery was planned during the summer of 1963 and so on. Incredibly, it is the first proper review and investigation of the facts by a senior detective who has no vested interest in holding up the initial investigation as full or complete. The assistance of one of the train robbers has added greatly to that process.

ONE

YOUR KEY WITNESS

Much of what follows requires you to suspend belief in the integrity of the police in the late 1950s and early '60s, the nature and extent of violent crime during that period and any long-held conclusions about the Great Train Robbery (GTR). Your doing so will depend on your thinking me a credible witness. Here is my brief CV.

I was brought up on council estates in the 1940s, '50s and '60s and had a working-class childhood. I left school without any qualifications and as a 'nearly' professional footballer, took various labouring jobs on building sites.

All the teenagers I hung out with had criminal convictions. One later committed suicide in prison at a young age, having killed his wife; another was sentenced for armed robbery. I smoked pot, popped a few pills, got into scraps and got drunk too often. That was all very typical of someone from my background.

Nearing my 19th birthday and having met a 'straight' and beautiful young woman, I decided I needed to change my ways in order not to frighten her off. No more drunkenness, drugs, or silliness. I joined the Transport Police at Southampton Docks. I scraped in.

I had never studied before, but now I had to. Failure to pass the necessary police exams would have meant my being 'required to resign'. That was an outcome I was determined to avoid at all cost. Exams aside, I achieved an excellent arrest record and was moved into CID at the remarkably young age of 21.

I was promoted to sergeant at the age of 23 and transferred to London. From there I was gradually promoted up to the rank of detective superintendent, aged 42. There I stayed.

By the time of my retirement I had received numerous commendations from Old Bailey judges, chief constables, and one from the Director of Public Prosecutions as well as the thanks of about three government ministers.

I formed two public charities and was the main author of the first ACPO Code of Ethics for Policing and one of the writers of the ACPO Murder Manual (the bit on corporate killing).

I led many high-profile investigations and was a Director of Studies at the National Police Staff College, Bramshill. I won two scholarships to university and was invited to apply for a Fulbright Scholarship to the USA.

I served for eight years as the detective superintendent for British Transport Police (BTP) and was head of CID. In that capacity I received, many years after the first, a commendation for my part in the detection of an organised gang of dangerous mail train robbers following a multi-million-pound theft.

The record shows that I took on police corruption head first. Before retiring, I received police long-service and good-conduct awards. Frustrated at my bosses, I left the police service as soon as my pension became payable at 50. I immediately joined the Microsoft Corporation in a senior capacity based at its European headquarters in Paris.

After that I had a series of senior corporate positions including director at the world's second largest pharmaceutical company, GlaxoSmithKline. Before leaving there, I was highlighted for promotion to vice-president. During that time I conducted significant international investigations into organised crime and the counterfeiting of medicines.

I have had two books published, the first on counterfeit medicines and organised crime. That led to my giving expert testimony before the United States' Senate. The second, a memoir, was described in *The Guardian* as being, 'The best of the genre' (police memoirs). I am a law graduate and Fellow of the Royal Society of Arts. I have been married since 1968.

TWO

THE GREAT TRAIN ROBBERY

Tom Wisbey told me that if everyone who had claimed to have taken part in the robbery, or been invited to, were to get together, you could fill Wembley Stadium.

We have had many GTR books and films claiming 'exclusive' access to the truth, but many are pure fantasy. More recently we have been expected to believe that Bruce Reynolds was the 'Mr Big'. In reality, as I will show, he was perhaps more 'Mr Big Ego'.

Within hours of the robbery, the Post Office publicised a £10,000 reward for information leading to the arrest of those involved. In addition, the loss adjusters for the banks offered £25,000.

That was enough to buy seven family houses in London. Can you imagine what professional informers, casual 'grasses', other thieves, bent coppers, 'cheeky chappies' and various chancers would have done to get a share of that?

Take a simple example that might ultimately have led to a great deal of trouble. In an official memorandum, which seems to have been taken very seriously by the Post Office Investigation Department and their bosses, information which they have received states:

At 9.10 p.m. on the 8th August (1963) an open Mini bus drew up outside 99, Pollards Hill South, Norbury … It contained about thirty pillowcases – stripped [sic] ticking – and each of them was filled with something or other and each had its neck tied with string or rope … Two men were in the (open topped) mini-bus and … the men took the pillowcases, together with some sacks or bags, into the house.

Apparently, this was regarded as significant because the informant knew that the woman who lived in the house had at some stage been a prostitute. As if that wasn't enough to seal her fate as part of the GTR gang, the informant reveals that 'she once lived with a man who was convicted of violence'!

The apparent intrigue deepens: 'There are two friends who call frequently at the house – a blond woman and a balding man, middle-aged.' The official memorandum is concluded with the solemn instruction, 'We would look into the possibility that the pillow cases might have contained some of the proceeds of the mail train robbery.' It is signed by a C. Osmond.

Now, you might think it ever so slightly unlikely that the implications of this would be taken seriously. That, having pulled off the biggest robbery in history just a few hours earlier, and with news of the event being broadcast every hour into homes across the country, the bone-headed robbers have loaded the money into pillow cases and conveyed it across London in an open-topped vehicle.

You might think it sounds like part of a script for an Ealing comedy. But does that stop the intrepid Post Office Investigation Department Controller taking this nonsense seriously? Clearly not. And worse, does it stop him from taking the story to a meeting with Metropolitan Police Commander Hatherill and various chief constables and the most senior police investigators? No.

But taking the issue seriously does provide the notion of someone in Norbury being involved, as well as a middle-aged balding man and a blonde (you could never trust a blonde in those days; all blondes were by definition and common consent 'hussies').

Many years later, the description of a middle-aged balding man with a connection to that part of London was resurrected and built upon by Gordon Goody to result in the false identification of the man who gave the necessary inside information. He was thereafter called the 'Ulsterman'.

To be clear, I am not saying the unlikely tale of the '30 pillow cases with stripped [sic] ticking' should have been ignored.

No, first it should have been evaluated and then prioritised (as non-urgent). Instead of that, as is clear from the records, it was treated as very significant and urgent. The result seems to have been numerous wasted man-hours.

When the first draft of this book was nearly complete, a journalist read it and checked references for me. He found in one of the books I had referred him to, reference to the '30 pillowcases full of money' story, and chose to accept it without question. He thought it must have been a significant investigative lead. A few days later when we met I asked him if he really thought anyone with half a brain would ever think it was a good way to transport a huge number of banknotes, particularly in those circumstances.

He responded by saying that the words 'pillowcases' had not been mentioned at all in the book referred to; instead it referred, he said, to 'bags or sacks or something'. He went on to say that no open-topped van had been mentioned either. He was 100 per cent wrong.

However, I'm certain he was not trying to deceive me, so what was going on? Nothing more I think than a subconscious desire to accept an underlying theory that would have been useful for his purposes, rather like that Post Office official, Mr Osmond.

Writing this book entailed reading as much as I could about the subject and then stripping away as much nonsense as possible. That process has helped me to ignore conventional and accepted conclusions and bring out the truth. Some of that has been easy to do, some of it very hard. One strong example is the position of the much respected and admired Train Driver Mills.

For many years I fulfilled the role of senior investigating officer in cases involving serial rapists, homicide, kidnapping, armed robberies and other serious crime. There is always a need to take the same fundamental approach. It is to start with the false assumption that anyone could have committed the crime. No one is too cherished, too rich, or too powerful to be presumed incapable.

The most perfect example in our case would be to consider whether the train driver, his Second Man (assistant), train guard or signalman on duty in the relevant signal box were criminally involved. Hard to believe though it is, this does not appear to have been the case in 1963. It is a particularly sensitive matter in relation to Driver Mills, but you will see the outcome is not straightforward by any means.

As a result of the above, this book sheds fresh light on key issues in the case and provides a fresh perspective. I have not performed a proper 'cold case review' (my resources are now restricted to a single set of less-than-perfect eyes and my knowledge of police procedures are twenty years out of date). But if this were a formal review then there is no doubt that 'fresh lines of enquiry' have been revealed.

I was a railway detective for a long time. I saw and heard a lot of things that you will think improbable. There were policemen who would routinely steal, 'fit people up', and one or two who were even prepared to kill – and I mean murder other policemen or criminals who stood in their way. 'Murder other policemen'; that sounds fanciful, but I personally came across 'threats to kill' on two occasions, once within the Metropolitan Police and once within my own force, the Transport Police. In neither case was there ever an official investigation.

Telling you that, in the 1960s and 1970s, some detectives from the Met were corrupt will not surprise you. Some got rich, but that shouldn't be news to you either. What you might not know is how that corruption in the London police forces (Met and City of London) extended to the Transport Police and, of course, beyond.

In the late 1970s a number of detectives from the Transport Police received long prison sentences for organising the theft of lorry loads of goods from the Bricklayers Arms Depot in South London. Not long before, a senior detective had been punished for doing likewise at the railway yards in Stratford, East London. I mention that now because shortly I will be asking you to consider a railway policemen was involved in the GTR.

The Great Train Robbery has entered folklore as the story of likeable rogues who used cunning and daring to get rich and get one over on the State in a largely non-violent way. These days the media describe the perpetrators as (variously) hairdressers, florists, carpenters, window cleaners, club owners and bookmakers.

I think at least some who have made those claims have done so honestly but, more importantly, in complete naivety.

Yes, the robbers created such nominal occupations for themselves. Gordon Goody did have a hairdressing business. Roger Cordrey did run a florist's shop, Tom Wisbey had a bookies and Bob Welch, for example, had a nightclub. I am even prepared to believe that Jim Hussey cleaned the odd window (but not often). Essentially, these adopted occupations were firstly to provide an 'excuse' for having money in their pockets. Secondly, when arrested or put before the courts, it gave the impression that they were something other than professional lawbreakers.

The mythology surrounding the robbery has largely been written by the popular press. It has been created and added to by the robbers themselves, their families and sycophants. But it might also have been fuelled by those with an interest in holding onto any remains of the outstanding fortune; after all, the vast bulk of the money is still missing – in today's terms there is still over £40 million missing.

According to myth, the train robbers belonged to the days when villains were 'honourable' and policemen were 'honest and upright'; professional villains generally left ordinary people alone; 'good' villains never informed on one another and they rarely used violence. In that mythical world, violent crime was hardly ever encountered. A quick look at the current extraordinary levels of knife crime tells a different story. Levels of stabbing have not been as high as they are now since the 1940s and 1950s.

Similarly, the use of firearms in the furtherance of theft is today nowhere near the level it was in 1950s and '60s. And it is the same with 'murder in the furtherance of crime' (leaving aside acts of terrorism).

At the same time during that mythical halcyon period, policemen were honest, upright, trustworthy individuals. They would never tell lies in the witness box. They would never take bribes. They were almost invariably dedicated public servants who thought little for their own health, wealth or safety. It was apparently a world of *Dixon of Dock Green* and thieves who would mutter 'It's a fair cop guv' at the mere sight of a uniform. There might be some comfort in seeing the world of our youth in that way, but it truly never was like that.

Those involved in the GTR were violent, determined criminals and many of them had previous convictions for wounding, grievous bodily harm, armed robbery and other serious crimes. In reality, while people watched 'Dixon' on the telly, police corruption was rife. Many of the Met CID and Transport Police CID were routinely corrupt. Many of the worst criminals were 'looked after' by senior detectives, for the sake of continued liberty on the one hand and on the other for the sake of personal financial gain. They might seem like harsh comments but as I show later, police corruption was the norm.

However, let me say for the sake of completeness that it was never the case of the odd 'rotten apple'. In reality, a significant number of senior officers were obtaining illicit gains from corrupt relationships with criminals. Other senior officers who were not 'on the take' either encouraged their subordinates to get results at any cost, or simply stood by and did nothing.

I have been asked whether, in this book, I am defining police 'corruption' by today's standards. The answer to that is yes; after all, your interpretation of events, and mine, are a natural reflection of the times we live in. But I would also say that corruption as defined today, is really not that different to corruption as defined then. Thinking hard about it, how do today's police ethics compare with those of the late 1950s and '60s? I can say with certainty, upon reflection, I really don't know.

Since the GTR of 1963 we have had a continuous series of false accounts that have been accepted as true and built upon. The robbers themselves have played more than their fair part in that. Once we were told that some mysterious former Second World War Nazi officer organised the whole thing, then there was that alleged South African involvement. According to another version of events, it was all the work of a mysterious chess-playing hermit who lived in a small flat above a small shop in Brighton. Apparently, said hermit wasn't interested in the money; it was the challenge of 'the game'. We have also had a solicitor nominated as the mastermind. Do you remember that tale about a member of the House of Lords setting it all up? I used to think that anyone with an IQ in double figures would not swallow much of it. Now I'm really not so sure.

I guess it must have been inevitable once a bunch of thieves and dubious journalists realised they could get easy money by making 'revelations'. The ever-present need to generate interest and excitement was bound to lead to absurdity being added to nonsense. Add to that writers who were genuinely keen to either generate a fresh angle on the story, or simply make a 'name', and you have a recipe for further exaggeration and misinterpretation.

This book was written after I had studied many accounts including confidential police files, books, articles, newspapers and broadcast materials created over many years. But it is not just meta-analysis; this work has been done, and assisted, by individuals who know the actual terrain much better than most. Having spent the last few years reading much of what has been written, I am struck by one overwhelming conclusion: lies have become myths and the myths have become reality.

The last GTR YouTube video I watched was in January 2019. It was the final straw; I could only manage to tolerate the first five minutes. In that time one very famous TV presenter declared that the 'Jewel thief, Bruce Reynolds' was 'the mastermind'. Then he introduced an expert who seemed to have no apparent expertise in crime or detection and knew so little about the GTR that he stated that the robbery 'Took place at 4 a.m.'

As I will show you, Reynolds was not the mastermind, or even the foreman. The robbery, as is widely known, took place shortly after 3 a.m. By 4 a.m. the crooks were 27 miles away, back at Leatherslade Farm.

Another painful account is given in the film featuring Gordon Goody, shortly before he died. Goody allegedly (but very mistakenly) unmasks and identifies the Post Office insider, the 'Ulsterman'. Later in this book I show that to be rubbish. But in one recreated scene in that film, masked men are seen standing over Driver Mills as, under duress, he moves the stricken train forward. The actor playing Mills is wearing a very clean and professionally bound bandage over his head wound. There is no sign of blood or terror. The subliminal message is both obvious and wrong: 'the robbers were really concerned about the unfortunate injury to Mills and made sure that it was properly attended to.'

Of course, a moment's reflection indicates that they could not possibly have made sure proper first aid was given, even if they had the desire and time to do so. But evidently someone involved in that production chose not to show a semi-conscious Mills, terrified into moving his train, in pain, with blood coursing from his scalp across his face and neck. In other words they were not prepared to show the truth. Why? Presumably because, well, we all know the robbers were really just jovial chaps, who really meant no harm to anyone.

Many of the books I have read (never mind those YouTube videos) have been silly. Many have been full of provable errors. I won't bother you further with those. The vast majority of accounts fail completely to understand how it is to be a professional villain, or a professional detective, and some fundamentally misunderstand the relationship between those two roles.

I have ignored much of the nonsense spread by some broadcasters and writers. However, some of the misinformation, particularly the books by robbers Goody and Reynolds, needs to be shown as false in order to arrive at the truth.

Let me say first that I am not, and never have been, interested in joining any sort of clique in which individuals avoid all criticism of fellow members, whether it be freemasons, local pub crowd, occupational group or whatever. God knows society has been damaged enough by that approach. So, in what I have already said, and have yet to say, there is criticism of the police, British Railways, the Post Office and others.

I should also say there are three books on the Great Train Robbery that stand head and shoulders above most and I refer to them frequently hereafter. They are:

The Robbers' Tale by Peta Fordham. The author had access to at least two of the robbers during and after the main trial in 1964. In addition, she witnessed the whole trial and heard all the evidence. It is essential reading for that reason alone. As you will see later, it provides a somewhat romanticised description of the characters involved and for me that detracts, but it is nevertheless very informative. I refer to it simply as 'Peta Fordham's book' or 'Fordham' or *The Robbers' Tale*.

Secondly, *The Great Train Robbery – Crime of the Century – The Definitive Account* by Nick Russell-Pavier and Stewart Richards. I found this the most comprehensive and rounded view of all. If there is a single book that needs to be read to understand the Great Train Robbery, this is it. From now on, for the sake of brevity I'll refer to *Crime of the Century* or 'Russell-Pavier/Richards'.

Thirdly, *The Great Train Robbery – The Untold Story from the Closed Investigation Files* by Andrew Cook. Henceforth, I'll say 'Cook' or *The Untold Story*. No one can doubt the thoroughness of Mr Cook's research. This is a very detailed account with particular reference to the Post Office Investigation Department (POID) papers. Many of the POID's documents had been kept confidential for many years, and Cook examines these, and other more recently 'released' documents, methodically. I found this book extremely valuable as a source of reference.

The Post Office staff involved in the GTR investigation, just like those of other agencies no doubt, obviously wished to show themselves in the best possible light, and this is reflected in the Post Office papers that Cook used. However, in truth, the Post Office Investigation Department was not, in my experience, a meat-eating, testosterone-driven, results-focused band of experienced, hard-nosed detectives.

They were generally intelligent, generally hard-working, reliable, amiable investigators. They did not undergo detective training and they had no powers of arrest. At the 'sharp end' they concerned themselves with investigations into dishonest postmen. Sometimes, they would do joint observations with Transport Police detectives. But I can say without hesitation and with absolute provable certainty, it was always the BTP men who 'felt the collar' of anyone found stealing mail. If that person happened to be a postman, then courtesy demanded that the case was put in the hands of the POID. If anyone is yet to read Mr Cook's excellent and extremely well-researched book, they should bear that in mind. In addition – and this has nothing to do with Mr Cook's reporting – with the right mindset, you will see a definite naivety in some of the records made by Post Office staff during the GTR investigation in addition to that one already mentioned (pillowcases full of money!).

This account of the Great Train Robbery is the first by an experienced senior Transport Police detective. Working with the vital information that I gained from Tom Wisbey, which he gave cautiously, I measured it against my own prior knowledge and then checked it against the printed words of others. I have no axe to grind; I have no police action, or misdeed, to cover up, defend or celebrate. This book both exposes falsehoods and reveals new information. It gives greater insight than ever before as to the identity of the mastermind. No, it wasn't Bruce Reynolds. It completely debunks the modern notion that the insider (aka 'The Ulsterman') was Patrick McKenna, a now-deceased Manchester postman. And it reveals who else was definitely or probably involved, i.e. a policeman, a railway man, a bookmaker, a robber.

In recent years, the name Danny Pembroke has been referred to as one of the robbers that got away. The pages that follow explain for the first time how Danny Pembroke became involved, and his relationship with Tom Wisbey, who also revealed to me, for the first time, the name of another train robber: Freddie Sansom. He was a man whose family had been close to Tom's for a lifetime.

There has been acceptance of the notion that the key 'insider' was a man who became known as the 'The Ulsterman'. The accepted 'truth' is a classic example of an irrelevant fact being built into a broader fictitious assertion. I will show you proof enough to convince a jury that this is complete fabrication and a cynical way to protect the guilty and exploit the innocent.

But what if other significant lies have been told to protect other guilty parties? Well, the most contentious parts of this book deal precisely with those issues. One obvious example is that a Transport Police detective might have been the 'insider'.

The facts published in this book were intended to form the basis of a novel I was writing with the help of Tom Wisbey. After Tom's death, I eventually became convinced that it was right to try to extract the fact from the fiction, hence this book. But I still strongly agree with the person who wrote:

> No one is more conscious than I of the gaps in the story. The trouble is that, in setting out to report truthfully, one is at a great disadvantage. Fictional characters can be made to speak at the right moment: real life ones cannot and they forget and invent. [*]

I know that some of you will suspect that only a bent copper could get close to a gangster like Tom Wisbey. The truth is that criminals hate bent policemen, for like most dishonest people, bent policemen are of course untrustworthy.

You will see the word 'gangster' appear a lot in this book. But what does that word really mean? I have used it as an easy way to recreate in the reader's mind the sense of those professional criminals who take part in a serious joint criminal enterprise (gang) and use violence and intimidation to that end. But that is all. The train robbers, those who were caught, were truly violent thieves, but not members of any sort of mafia. On the other hand, as you will see, if we were looking to find behind the GTR any real sense of organised criminal structure then we would not have to look far.

'Mr Big', as I will show later, wasn't just a thief. He had a fluid but very real 'open-ended' organisation that operated internationally. His work encompassed many aspects of serious crime from which he gained and retained substantial wealth.

Having spoken above about my disdain for membership of any clique, I must tell you that Tom Wisbey and I were from the same tribe. What does that mean? Well it doesn't mean that I was born or brought up in London, or ever belonged to a gang of professional thieves. A few years ago, I saw a front-page newspaper picture of the Queen under a headline that read something like 'Chief of our Tribe'. But if you look at the shenanigans of some of the Royal Family, you might question whether even they,

---

[*] Fordham, *The Robbers' Tale*, Preface.

though related by blood or marriage, are part of the same tribe as she. I can hear you say, 'Of course they are.'

Well, it's the same with members of the working-class tribe. Tom had no pretensions of being anything other than what he was. He came from a metropolis, a council house and an average working-class family. That I can absolutely relate to more than I ever possibly could to any 'middle', aristocratic or royal class: these are different tribes. The best values of ordinary working-class families are self-reliance, hard work, devotion to family, lack of greed, modesty and courage. Tom was a tribe member that strayed badly; he was the self-confessed black sheep of the family.

How is that relevant to the worth of what you are reading? Well, I understand the tribe and its language and norms in a way that the typical reporter, barrister or middle-class writer never could. Anyone who believes that inside themselves there is no potential killer, no potential thief, knows little about themselves. Without understanding your own potential for wrongdoing, you are unlikely to understand it in others. So, this book is written from within.

After Tom died, I put my entire research and draft novel to one side. I had done, and was doing, lots of other creative writing. Some time later, I took advice from a man I have known since we both played in the snow together as children in the streets of the winter of 1962, Andy Jordan. He told me that of all the writing projects I had on my desk, the GTR one was the most interesting. Thereafter I got back down to finishing the novel: first as a six-part TV script, then on the good advice of my agent as a two-part TV drama.

Then my phone rang. Channel 4 asked me to help them with a documentary that was planned about counterfeit medicines (that's a whole different story) and I agreed to help. When I got to know the people I was dealing with there I told them about how Tom and I had worked together and the revelations. They showed an immediate interest and the story was easily commissioned. The process of persuading them of the validity of my claims was not easy. In fact, it was very frustrating, but I am assured it was also 'totally necessary'.

I had not previously shared the contents of the book with anyone. They were rightly sceptical and interviewed numerous people to check the facts I claimed and the assertions I had made. Repeatedly they came back telling me that this 'expert' and that 'writer' didn't agree with much that I had written. I had to point out to them that this book completely upsets the status quo. It means that those same experts have been wrong to believe much of the rubbish that has been peddled and failed to have spotted some of these 'truths' for themselves.

Having put that frustration behind me, I can now say that the Channel 4 verification process has proven useful. Because now I can say, with some confidence, that few or no other accounts have undergone such scrutiny. Every assertion of fact has had to be tested and I am sure this has led to a better book.

THREE

THE CROWN V. GENTRY & OTHERS 1982

In 1981, I was a young detective inspector, just 31, who had just been transferred to BTP Headquarters CID. I had maintained a good level of arrests throughout my service, but my last posting had ended painfully and abruptly. I was the detective inspector responsible for the railways in East London, parts of Essex and East Anglia, and the patch included the largest 'inland port' in the country, Stratford International Freight Terminal.

After a long series of thefts of and from valuable containers, I mounted a weekend operation. My team and I raided a number of premises in the East End, arrests were made, and a good deal of property was recovered. To my complete dismay, my boss reacted with aggression. The accusations made against me were both serious and false, and trivial and true.

I was suspended from duty and my warrant card and keys to police buildings were taken from me. I was to make no contact with other police staff. And of course, I had no idea what I was supposed to have done wrong. Suspending a police officer from duty is a rare event, only done when criminal charges and dismissal are likely to follow. Suspending a detective inspector is even rarer and more ominous.

Eventually I discovered that the false allegations were that I had assaulted a prisoner and made a false written statement of evidence. The true ones were that I had made an accurate entry in two of my officers' official CID diaries that purported to have been made by them. It was clear that for some reason unknown to me, 'the knives had been out'.

In the end, the truth was told and the serious charges dropped (and I was simply given a formal caution for the trivial offences). But I was also transferred from that post on the basis that I could not be expected to work further in that environment. I was moved to HQ CID, the department expected to deal with the most serious crimes that affected the railways. I was delighted.

I found the department was divided into three teams, one of which was a dedicated mailbag squad. When I arrived, a very busy detective inspector, John MacDonnell, was running the team successfully. As had been the case as far back as anyone could remember, the mailbag squad's regular business involved the investigation and detection of professional thieves. In addition they also dealt with rail staff and postmen who were light-fingered enough to steal the odd mailbag.

But while that team was occupied with too many cases, the theft of mailbags continued, and the value of such crimes was escalating. Sometimes a million pounds' worth of property would be stolen in one hit.

It wasn't long before a certain woman found her way into a Met. police station and made it known that she wanted to speak to the Transport Police CID. The call found its way to me and within a few hours this attractive woman, Tina Meer, was telling me a remarkable story involving her live-in lover Billy Gentry, Charlie Kray, other members of the old Kray 'Firm', former Great Train Robbers Tom Wisbey and Bill Hussey, and other well-known gangsters.

She said they had all been involved in the organised and continuing theft of high-value mails from trains. She described how late at night Billy Gentry would arrive home and empty a suitcase in her flat in Islington. She told us about the green canvas bags that were dumped from the suitcase onto the carpet. How he would then cut them open with an electric carving knife and expose the gems, travellers' cheques, wages and other valuables that they held.

I had two bosses, Alan Botwood (DCI – Detective Chief Inspector) and Maurice Woodman (DCS – Detective Chief Superintendent). Alan had arrived at headquarters at about the same time as me. He was from Wales, a proud and upright man. But so far as we could tell, he had never been an operational detective. In any event, Alan was instructed by the DCS to organise for Tina to be taken to a place of safety and ensure that from that moment she was guarded twenty-four hours a day.

My job was equally specific. I was to start an immediate investigation to establish the truth of Tina's story, then to build 'intelligence packages' on every suspect identified by those investigations. Subsequently, my job was to build those intelligence packages into 'search and arrest dockets' and finally to build a case for the prosecution.

The DCS oversaw Tina's care, kept the top bosses reassured and, most importantly, ensured that adequate resources were allocated to both Alan Botwood and me. I hope to avoid the use of the word 'me' for the rest of this chapter at least. I would most certainly have failed pretty quickly had it not been for the team I had around me. I could still name them all, but that would bore you. But Steve Craske, one of my detective sergeants, was my right-hand man (even though during the course of the twelve-month investigation he tried to decapitate me by launching a typewriter at me in frustration).

Martin Leadbetter, a senior fingerprint officer with the Hertfordshire Constabulary who examined well over £2 million worth of travellers' cheques and obtained numerous 'positive idents' is another man who did so much to ensure the case was properly made.

Another was Detective Sergeant Peter Bennett from C11 (Intelligence Branch) at New Scotland Yard. How lucky I was to have him. Peter was such a well-informed, helpful, trusting and trustworthy ally. Without Peter our work would have been exposed to the corrupt element at the Yard and the villains tipped off. Without Peter some or all of the criminal intelligence on all these rogues would have been hidden from us.

I had so much to learn about all of these infamous villains who were somehow linked, it seemed, to both the Kray fraternity and the GTR. I requested and received the complete Met Police Great Train Robbery investigation file and every suspect's C11 file. (Major criminals were each subject of an individual file, created and held by C11 – the Intelligence Department at New Scotland Yard.)

By the way, I say 'Great Train Robbery file' but in reality, it was at least a cubic yard comprising hundreds of files. I studied as much of the relevant material as I could. The papers disclosed that Bill Gentry, a notorious armed robber, had also been a close associate of Reggie and Ronnie Kray, and had run the El Morocco nightclub for them. One of our other prisoners had run the Krays' protection rackets. Other details important to the story I'm telling you now were also revealed, but I'll tell you those in context as the book unfolds.

When I had finished managing all the necessary ground work, BTP Force headquarters CID officers (armed and unarmed), backed up by BTP divisional detectives, uniform staff and dog-handlers, and supported by specialist firearms units from the Met, carried out simultaneous arrests and premises searches.

In all, some twenty-one individuals were eventually charged. Billy Gentry was amongst them. Billy, aka 'Billy G' was known at Criminal Records Office under the surname 'Newman', which he gave upon his first arrest. Gentry's considerable CRO file was thus forever labelled with that name.

Amongst the other well-known professional lawbreakers were Tom Wisbey, who was out of prison on licence, and one Dodger Mullins, who had been robbing Post Office and mail trains blind since the Second World War!

Bill Gentry had all the trappings of his criminal status. He had a great deal of physical 'presence' and dressed like a 1950s movie star – bespoke Savile Row suits, finest shirts, silk ties, Italian leather shoes. He drove a beautiful classic Mercedes convertible sports car and usually had a beautiful woman by his side. He was one of the most famous villains in London and, like Wisbey, he shunned publicity, but to those 'in the know' he was taken very seriously.

On the night of the arrests, Wisbey, Gentry and other prisoners were brought to our new premises at Tavistock Place in Bloomsbury. Our official moving-in date was several weeks away, but we needed space, security and communications, and the building was perfectly suited. However, the premises were so unfinished that there were no signs on the walls and, of course, no other staff in the building. It was not even fully furnished. I found out thirty years later that the prisoners thought they had been whisked off to some top-secret location (more of that later).

Wisbey was actually brought in by Detective Sergeant Steve Craske (referred to above) and his team, then formally questioned under caution by Woodman and Botwood. Of course, he admitted nothing. I felt, rightly or wrongly, that my interviewing skills were better than theirs and so persuaded DCS Woodman to let me have a go. I tried my best using all the best legal means, but he said nothing. I'll admit now, in desperation I threatened, unlawfully, to 'verbal him' (claim falsely that he had made admissions of guilt). His reaction to my threat surprised me. He said to me, 'I don't think you'll fit me up. You don't strike me as that sort of person Mr Satchwell.' And he was right.

That day, his wife Renee Wisbey came to visit him. She brought their surviving daughter, Marilyn (Marilyn's twin had been tragically killed in a car crash while Tom was imprisoned some years earlier). Renee Wisbey was about 50 at the time, stylish, engaging and pleasant.

Within days, part of my role as the officer in charge of the case was to look after all the applications before the court to keep those we had arrested in custody. (There was no Crown Prosecution Service in those days.) Tom Wisbey made repeated attempts to get bail. I fought every one successfully at both magistrates' court and at the High Court in The Strand.

The period between arrests and trial extended well over a year, and I had been busy in that time ensuring the case was watertight. By the time of the trial, Tom Wisbey and I knew one other. After a three-month trial at court no. 2 at the Old Bailey, all but one

1982 after the Old Bailey trial, Tom Wisbey and his wife, Renee.

of twenty-one prisoners (one David Potter) were found guilty. Some got substantial periods of imprisonment.

Potter was an unusual man. I have interviewed literally hundreds of prisoners over the years, but only one other had the characteristic that I saw when I questioned him. He was already serving a very long sentence and I interviewed him in prison. He came into the interview room, sat opposite and with a hateful expression stared out from 'dead' eyes. I introduced myself and he remained silent. I tried to engage in a little small talk. Nothing. I asked him several opening questions. Nothing. I started again, more small talk. Nothing. Nothing. There wasn't a thing I could do to get him to even acknowledge my presence, not a word nor nod of the head.

One of those who received (yet another) long prison sentence was Bill Gentry. As is normal, after he had been sentenced (eight and a half years if I remember correctly), I went to see him in the cells under the 'Bailey'.

You have to understand that Gentry was a hard man; his last arrest had resulted in one of the arresting officers being awarded the George Medal and the other the George Cross.*

In that case Gentry had been working with the man regarded as 'Public Enemy Number One' – John McVicar. Gentry and McVicar, following an armed robbery, had been chased by unarmed police officers across London. The two uniformed Met police officers narrowly escaped death time and time again as more than fifteen shots were fired into their car. The story didn't end there, and it is a remarkable one of police bravery.

Gentry's long criminal record showed that he was not only an extremely violent gangster but that he never pleaded guilty and never voiced anything but anger towards policemen. My point in telling you all that? Well, Gentry, that morning in the cells, after he had just been 'weighed off' and was about to return to his familiar diet of porridge, spoke to me calmly. Earlier, I had given evidence to the court of his bad character and I had indicated he was the ringleader of the gang. His exact words to me in the cell that day were, 'You think I'm number one; I'm not even number six.'

There was little doubt in my mind that he was indicating that there was an organisation behind the mailbag thefts that no one had ever dreamed of. Was it, as they say, 'a wind up'? I can't be sure, but one thing I do know, Gentry was not a man to joke, and even the most comical character would not have felt jolly at that moment – particularly towards me.

Unlike on the telly, the detective work doesn't stop once an arrest is made, and during the period between the arrests and the subsequent trial, as I have already indicated, there was a mountain of work to be done to prove our case.

When I was an enthusiastic 19-year-old constable, I wheeled yet another prisoner into the CID office. An old and shrewd

---

* See *London Gazette* of Friday, 19 May 1967.

detective called Ron Gilmore sat me down and gave me some fatherly advice. This is what he said:

> An old lion hunter invited a young, inexperienced friend to accompany him on his next expedition. When they arrived in the jungle the young man couldn't wait to hunt lions. 'Hold on,' said the older man, 'let's make camp, check our equipment and start out fresh in the morning when we are fully prepared.'
>
> The next morning the young man was up and dressed before it was light. Armed with his rifle and a torch, he set off alone into the bush. About thirty minutes later the older man was awoken by shouts from outside the tent, he roused himself and peered out. His young friend was racing back to the tent chased by a lion. As the older man watched, the lion launched itself at the young man. Just in time to avoid injury, the young man ducked and the lion sailed straight over him and into the tent with the old boy.
>
> The young man immediately shouted towards the tent, 'You deal with that one and I'll go and find another!'

The point was well made. It is easy to arrest someone, but that is when the real work of proving the case begins. When it comes to lions and professional gangsters they are not easily overcome. And so it proved: veiled and not so veiled threats against witnesses; an attempt to interfere with exhibits via a break at our police exhibits store; I was offered a considerable amount of money not to oppose bail; and shady characters turned up at the Detective Chief Superintendent's office with a view to 'explaining certain things'. Furthermore, our supergrass demanded to be allowed to meet another gangster who had got word to her that he wanted to discuss 'her position' with her.

At the same time we continued to seek other 'lions': Jim Hussey was questioned and released (insufficient evidence); Charlie Kray was sought (we couldn't find him); John McVicar turned up in my office representing Billy Gentry's interest. He was trying to get back the fabulous Mercedes we had seized (as the proceeds of crime) and so on.

While I had sole responsibility for that case, I was not relieved of other duties. Other gangsters from other cities including Glasgow were also stealing mails. In one case a young informant who had been assisting me was shot dead, executed, for his 'betrayal' (more of that later).

Simultaneously, I took a team of detectives to Manchester where we made several arrests of members of the infamous 'Quality Street Gang'. In addition, during that time, I built a relationship with another supergrass called John Moriarty, a violent man mountain and former minder for Charlie Kray. It was an intense time, but I was on top of my game and enjoyed it all.

That is the important backdrop to my next meeting with Tom Wisbey, thirty years later. But it is also the reason I received information that gave me my first suspicion about the identity of the GTR 'insider', the man who gave all the vital information to the 'Mr Big'.

The Gentry case was the BTP's first foray into arresting such a large gang of the most infamous gangsters. That is not to say they had not done terrific work of this kind before (as you will see), but it was rather a matter of scale. Such large-scale coordinated arrests against major crime figures were very rare in any police force and generally restricted to Flying Squad and Regional Crime Squad activity.

FOUR

THE RAILWAYS: A BEACON FOR THIEVES

To understand why the Great Train Robbery took place and the response, you have to know something of the context and why the robbery suited both robbers and crooked cops.

According to official figures, at the time of the GTR, the Post Office was transporting more than £4,000,000,000 (yes, £4 billion) a year, most of that by rail.* In addition to that vast sum, from Victorian times right up to the 1960s, huge amounts of valuable freight were carried by rail.

The railways, mailbags aside, were the main carriers of the most expensive consumer goods – perfume, cigarettes, spirits and so on. The railways had not yet suffered the 'Beeching axe' and the network of lines was much more extensive. In those days, road hauliers took only a small minority of the total traffic. For a very long period, the railways were the richest source of pickings for thieves. From the docks, everything from gold bullion, cigarettes and spirits to clothing and kitchen appliances was carried in railway wagons to all parts of the country – likewise things manufactured in Britain. In those days, before goods reached the shops, they would, unless produced locally, first have been stored in a railway depot or yard somewhere.

---

* Official Post Office file 120/95 as quoted in Cook, *The Untold Story*.

Mail had been carried by the railways since its earliest days. The last raid on a horse-drawn mail coach took place just north of Stoke at Congleton in 1839, where £5,000 was taken. The year before, the Railways (Conveyance of Mails) Act had been enacted and it required the railways to carry mails as directed by the Postmaster General. The records indicate that the move from 'highway and horse' to 'railways and steam' caused a temporary lull in the theft of mail in transit. However, within a year, a series of thefts of mails from trains commenced. That lucrative crime continued until the early 1990s when once again, the mails took to the roads.

During that 150-year period, most of the mail, including some of the very high-value packages, was carried in standard mail-bags alongside ordinary 'letter mail' in the train guard's 'cage' or 'brake'. But from early in the twentieth century and on until the 1990s, the railways also conveyed 'travelling post offices' (TPOs) – mobile post office sorting facilities aboard specially constructed carriages. Postmen working on the train would hastily open mailbags put on the TPO trains in the evening at, for instance, Southampton Central Railway Station. Individual letters and parcels were then expertly sorted into the right London postal delivery areas before the train arrived at London Waterloo.

That was the pattern night after night nationwide. Any highly valuable item sent by Royal Mail would be carried across the country either on ordinary passenger train or TPO. High-value thefts from the railways came in two types: theft from depots and theft of goods in transit. The nationalised railways were a pretty inefficient industry, and thus huge numbers of valuable parcels would go astray. Many, many millions of pounds' worth was stolen every year. In 1963 alone, for example, the British Transport Police arrested more than 7,000 people for theft and related offences (i.e. receiving).

Every day, across the country, some of the ordinary-looking mailbags would contain 'HV' (high value) bags. These contained a green canvas inner bag, within which were cash, jewellery, cheque books and other valuables. It was common for the high-value mailbags on an ordinary passenger train to carry items with the equivalent value of a modest house and sometimes a mansion and frequently very much more.

I know that some of what I have said already, all of which is provable, will have been rather surprising. But what I am going to explain now is more subtle but equally important to understanding why the train robbers thought they could get away with the Great Train Robbery.

When a crime is committed in Britain it is the duty of the local police force to report the fact to the Home Office (via the crime statistics). If a very serious crime is committed then the Home Office will 'liaise' with the force concerned so that the Home Office can answer questions that the Home Secretary might foresee being raised in the House of Commons, or indeed by the press.

However, if the crime is committed on the railways, the local police forces do not record it within their crime figures; they do not usually investigate it (though they might provide a 'first response') and the Home Office has no responsibility or answerability. Crime on the railways is the responsibility of the Transport Police and the reporting line to Government is via the Department of Transport. The Transport Police and the Home Office forces have different bosses. So, if a mailbag robbery occurs, or a train is unlawfully stopped or derailed, the local police can normally carry on regardless – they do not have to answer. It is simply not their problem (though in case of emergency when large numbers of police officers are required, other police forces have always responded generously).

It was certainly the case that in the 1950s, '60s and '70s, some corrupt Metropolitan police detectives would look the other way when crimes on the railways were committed, sometimes by those they were illegally in cahoots with. You can see the attraction, particularly if it meant that their 'manor' wasn't being targeted or their crime figures damaged.

The Metropolitan Police's Flying Squad, aka 'the Sweeney', 'the heavy mob' or 'C.8', was formed in the early twentieth century. Based at Scotland Yard, it comprised experienced 'hardcore' detectives and its fundamental remit was to arrest robbers (and pickpockets). By 1956, robberies were commonplace, and the squad was making thousands of arrests per year. However, during the years that followed, thanks to their efforts, armed robberies in the street (or 'across the pavement' in the parlance) were becoming more difficult for the robbers to commit without capture.

That was the environment that led to an escalating series of attacks on mail trains by hardened criminals and ultimately to the GTR.

In the early 1960s there was an escalating number of significant attacks on mail trains, most of them without violence. Each was reported by, and investigated by, the Transport Police. Only very rarely did the Home Office forces such as the Met have any operational input. The following figures were printed in the *Daily Express* as showing the escalation in 'Post Office crime':

1955–56	17 offences
1958–59	67 offences
1959–60	76 offences
1961–62	91 offences[*]

Sadly, the definition of 'Post Office crime' is not provided. But, given that the *Daily Express* was discussing the escalation in attacks on mail trains, it might reasonably be concluded that these figures refer to attacks on mail trains (but might include Post Office premises).

Yet the commonly held view is that the GTR was a 'one off'. Even the Post Master General told the world that prior to the Great Train Robbery the mails had been carried on trains without interruption for over 100 years. Was he speaking without thinking? That's very doubtful. Was he ignorant of the facts? Possibly, but unlikely. Was he trying desperately to manage his own position and claiming, 'I could not have foreseen this'? Probably. But whatever his motivation, his statement was true in only a very narrow sense.

---

[*]   Figures above are as quoted by Cook, *The Untold Story*, p.19.

It was true, however, so far as I can tell, that during the twentieth century no other TPO had been stopped mid-journey and subjected to a 'Wild West' style hold-up. But not all TPO trains were dedicated entirely to mail; some had passenger carriages too. These definitely had been repeatedly and violently attacked, as you will read later.

In addition, most Royal Mail high-value packages (HVPs) were carried with the ordinary mail within the guard's brake, or in the dedicated mail van of ordinary passenger trains. These had been successfully attacked on literally hundreds of occasions.

The blindness of seeing the GTR as a 'one off' means the crime is not seen as the culmination of earlier efforts, and not

Detective Inspector Kerr of the British Transport Police.

viewed as the result of lesser crimes going undetected. By looking at the crimes that built towards the eventual outcome (GTR) you arrive at a much better understanding of the GTR itself.

For instance, the *Daily Mirror* dated 21 January 1961 tells the story of a team of railway detectives (British Transport Police) who 'tailed' a known professional mail thief, called O'Malley, for three months and watched him as he, and his team, 'spotted' mail trains.

Eventually, the detectives, led by one Detective Inspector Bob Kerr (see page 51), lay in wait, hidden aboard the 'Irish mail train', en route from Euston to Holyhead (the mail was bound for Ireland, the train wasn't!). As the train sped through Tring (Hertfordshire), O'Malley and his gang, which included an 'all in' wrestler, broke into the guard's brake and set about stealing the registered mails. A fight broke out as the officers attempted to make arrests.

The detectives managed to overcome the robbers and arrest them. At their trial at the Old Bailey it was accepted that there had been fourteen successful attacks on the London–Midland train that year alone including five on the 'Irish mail train' (never mind all the other BR regions).

This is an interesting episode for more than one reason, for one of the convicted men was called Ronald Edwards, just like 'Buster'. He was of a similar age with a London address and committed exactly the same sort of crimes, with the same MO, on exactly the same railway lines as his more famous namesake.

FIVE

THE SOUTH COAST RAIDERS

As has already been made clear, mailbag thefts from trains had been occurring since the nineteenth century. However, from the mid-1950s to the time of the GTR, the annual number continued to grow steadily. But not only were the billions of pounds worth of property being increasingly attacked, so was the reputation of the Post Office.

It seemed that certain gangs could attack the mail trains at will, not by conventional hold-ups and not by stopping trains during the night in the middle of nowhere. There was simply no need to go to such lengths.

At one end of the spectrum, all an opportunist thief needed was the chance to snatch an unattended mailbag from a railway station. Many mailbags disappeared in this way, often from small-town railway stations where access and egress could be made quickly and without being seen. On several occasions at least, professional thieves would dress as postmen and simply carry a few bags away from a railway platform and place them in a van that had been altered to resemble a Post Office vehicle.

At the other end of the spectrum, professional thieves easily acquired the necessary BR issue keys to unlock the doors that connected the passenger coaches to the guard's brake and then to unlock the metal cage within. Once inside, thieves would quickly slice open the mailbags and dump any valuables into the suitcase they carried for the purpose. Work done, they would simply depart the train with other passengers, and, like other passengers, carry no more than a suitcase or two.

The more sensible thieves left no trace of their presence. Empty mail sacks and unwanted contents such as inexpensive gifts, wills and other legal documents would routinely be discarded from the moving train by being thrown from the window in the guard's brake door or be concealed beneath less valuable mailbags.

This would result in the theft not being noticed until the bags were counted from the train. Even then the location, nature and extent of the theft would not be known. No details of the stolen property would be available until individual victims complained that their parcel or envelope had not arrived. By these means, thieves could live very handsomely indeed. Individually or as gangs, they could go to work 'at will' with little risk of capture.

The BTP had a fairly small squad of men based in London who specialised in trying to catch mail thieves. But with hundreds of trains carrying high-value mail every day and all day and during the night, meaningful observations were extremely difficult. From about 1959 things got steadily worse and the attacks more serious.

On the afternoon of 18 August 1960, the 2.25 p.m. train left Brighton as usual. It was due to run non-stop to London Victoria. However, late in the journey the guard was attacked in the mail van. Three hooded robbers overwhelmed, blindfolded, gagged and bound him. Mailbags were slashed open and the high-value packages were put into a suitcase or two. When the train arrived at Victoria station, whilst the guard remained tied and bound, the three robbers walked calmly away from the train with £8,000 worth of registered mail. At that time, the average mail manual worker was earning about £10 a week.

Five weeks later, on a train heading in the opposite direction, another robbery occurred. As the Brighton-bound train ran between Hassocks and Preston Park, close to the Brighton end of the journey, three masked men again attacked the guard. This time, an accomplice stopped the train at a false red signal. The robbers ran from the train as the driver waited for the signal to change and went quickly to a nearby car and another successful getaway.

Early the next year, in January 1961, another high-profile attack took place, this time on a different Southern Region line.

The train was running between Waterloo and Teddington, just a few miles west, having left Waterloo at 9.47 p.m. When it stopped at Clapham Junction, just seven minutes after leaving Waterloo, a man in a wheelchair was lifted aboard and put into the mail brake with the guard. The wheelchair user's companion sat in a nearby compartment. (In those days wheelchair users had no choice but to travel in the guard's brake, the passenger train doors and corridors being too narrow for wheelchair use.)

The train moved off from Clapham and within minutes the apparently disabled passenger jumped from his wheelchair and attacked the guard. He then turned to the mailbags. As the train approached Earlsfield station it encountered an unexpected red signal and the train came to an unscheduled stop. Apparently, like a previous case, the red signal had been generated by the use of a 'track circuit clip'. This is a device used by railway workers to 'signal' to the staff at the signal box that the line is in use (e.g. during engineering works or an emergency). A red signal is then displayed.

The 'disabled' passenger and accomplice jumped from the stationary train with the contents of four high-value mailbags and ran across the railway lines to a nearby cemetery where a car was waiting. Within a minute, the robbers and loot had disappeared. This particular case was described to me first by Tom Wisbey; he had played the part of the wheelchair user's companion.

By 1961, the press was reporting on the success of the thieves on the Brighton line whom they had dubbed 'The Red Light Gang' and 'The South Coast Raiders'. It was clear that this gang had learned how to stop a train at signals without alerting signal boxes that something was amiss. Meanwhile at least one other gang, the Goody gang, was trying to do the same in other parts of the London area but without success.

It was during this period, again on the Brighton Line, that fire was used to steal from a train late at night. The fire was deliberately started in a rear passenger carriage as the train neared its next station stop. As it arrived at the station, the guard's attention was immediately called to it. Rail staff concentrated all their efforts on putting out the fire, minimising damage and, of course, getting the train moving again – you can imagine the excitement and distraction of it all. During all that lively activity, a gang of thieves made a thorough job of stealing the high-value mail from the guard's brake.

This was a well-known case and I put it to Tom Wisbey that his gang had used its usual 'creativity'. He frowned in response as if such a method of operation was beneath them. 'That wasn't us!' is all he would say, and I could see that getting a reputation as fire-raisers (with a penalty then of life imprisonment – Malicious Damage Act, 1861) would not have been a smart idea.

Needless to say, the South Coast Raiders were not the only ones 'working the Brighton Line' and nor did they restrict their activities to it. I know from my discussions with Tom Wisbey, and his relationship with Bill Gentry, Dodger Mullins and others, that the South Coast Raiders did not always go about their work in any sort of spectacular way. They would vary the time of day of the attack, the day of the week, the frequency and most importantly the MO.

The easiest method was simply to take unattended mailbags during the night as they were awaiting collection at a quiet railway station. I recall from the Metropolitan Police GTR files that the members of the Sansom family were known to have acquired Post Office uniforms, apparently for such purposes. On another occasion, just before midnight, The South Coast Raiders, dressed as railway men, removed £15,000 worth of valuables contained in mailbags as they were being offloaded at Brighton.

Sometimes they would divide forces, and half the team would hit a train in say Essex whilst the other half committed a theft in Kent. Sometimes a wheelchair would feature, sometimes they would simply grab and bind the guard. Usually they would simply nip into the guard's brake while the guard was busy elsewhere on the train. Then they would slit the mailbags, steal the goods, hide the debris and return to their first-class seats. They would leave the train as and when other passengers did.

When getaway cars were needed, they were always stolen within forty-eight hours of the planned raid and then burnt out to destroy any forensic evidence. Usually the Raiders used public transport as it was so much more anonymous, and a crowd is the perfect place to hide. Above all, the gang was cautious; they planned carefully and avoided any fanfare, they were discreet about their work and they rarely met together socially. No wonder they went completely undetected for years.

The South Coast Raiders originally consisted of the Harris brothers (you will almost certainly never have heard of them, and neither had I until Tom told me), Roger Cordrey, Danny Pembroke and Bob Welch. Others would come and go on an occasional basis too, the Sansom brothers and Jim Hussey for instance. Their leader was Danny Pembroke. In 1960, Danny invited his long-time friend, Tom Wisbey, to join the gang.

Roger Cordrey was not a gangster. He was an intelligent railway enthusiast who took his role extremely seriously. Sadly, he was also a gambling addict. He made it his business to become ever more expert in railway signalling, timetables and standard operating procedures. He was the Raiders' most valuable asset. He ran a florist shop in Brighton.

Sometime in mid or late 1962, Buster Edwards approached his old friend Tom Wisbey and requested the use of their technical expert, Roger Cordrey. That request was declined. Soon a second request was made that included the offer of the participation of all the Raiders in the big job that was being planned. There was reluctance on the part of the Raiders (they were doing very nicely and didn't need to expose themselves to unknown factors or have any desire to share Roger's expertise). But by some means they were persuaded to participate.

By December 1962, at the latest, there was a clear intention and sufficient manpower to rob the Glasgow–Euston TPO. This date can be fixed by several means, but first they needed a rehearsal (see Chapter 12).

POLICE CORRUPTION

All it takes for corruption to succeed is for good men to stand by and do nothing – which is precisely what good men usually do.

The history, nature, forms and extent of police corruption have never been fully appreciated by the majority of the British public. Any study of the early days of the Bow Street Runners will reveal it clearly in the very seeds from which the Metropolitan Police was formed in September 1829.

The best policemen have always come from the location and class they are policing. Without a close understanding of the social norms and vocabulary of a culture or subculture, effective policing is impossible and detecting crime particularly so.

Those who understand the language, structure and norms of the world of fine art can most effectively police the fight against theft and counterfeiting of fine art. Likewise, those crimes that are normally the province of the working class are best investigated by policemen who have no pretensions to be anything but that. There is a good deal of truth in the old maxim, 'Set a thief to catch a thief'. Although I would prefer 'Set someone who has the background shared by thieves, to catch a thief'.

So in Liverpool, London, Glasgow and elsewhere, on the streets, on the docks and on the railways, the uniform coppers who caught most thieves became CID officers. It is reasonable to conclude, therefore, that most of those CID men were rather closer to proving the maxim ('set a thief' etc.) than their uniform colleagues.

During the nineteenth century, the Metropolitan Police, with responsibility for catching thieves in by far the biggest and most

violent city in Britain, naturally developed a detective organisation and expertise that no other force could equal. It may have
been called a branch of the Met, but in reality, those plain-clothes
officers must have quickly begun to establish a separate identity
and their own rules of the game.

It soon became known by those who frequented the police
courts and police stations that the Metropolitan detective branch
was either corrupt in itself or, at best, peppered with corrupt
officers. (It has been proven more than once since those early
days that those who have greatest respect for the police, apart
from the police themselves, of course, are those that have least
contact with them.)

The Met has always had more than its fair share of the best
police officers. Sadly, it is undeniable that in both degree and
scale it has had more than its share of the worst too. Of course,
the great majority of officers fall into neither category.

In Victorian England, other towns and cities, large and small, also
saw the need to create their own plain-clothes departments. Many
of the biggest and some of the smallest of them recruited directly
from the corrupt capital. With that transfer of Metropolitan CID
staff went the seeds of endemic CID corruption.

By 1957 many police forces were both institutionally corrupt
and virtually untouchable. That year, following the arrest of its
chief constable, the Brighton force was described with grim
humour as 'The best police force money could buy'. The GTR
took place just six years later in the same policing environment,
years before the massive corruption cases at NSY that rocked
the Met.

My own policing experience started five years after the Great
Train Robbery. I started as a dock copper at Southampton.
Minor corruption was endemic; uniform constables would
take small bribes daily and routinely. Many detectives would
look after 'their' thieves and petty smuggling was the norm.
Meanwhile, more senior detectives were known to 'have their
own arrangements'. I remember one of the most senior police
officers at Southampton leaving the force abruptly: something
to do with firearms and alleged smuggling I seem to recall. The

Southampton Borough Force, which had recently been taken over by Hampshire Constabulary following a damning report by Her Majesty's Inspectorate of Constabulary, seemed to operate much in the same way as my own.

The influence of police corruption in all its various forms cannot be underestimated, both in the way it gradually undermines police organisations and in its more direct impact on particular cases. Detectives at all levels are still occasionally exposed as being in the employment of organised crime figures. This not only makes (because of leaks and tip-offs) the arrest of senior crime figures virtually impossible but causes harm to informants and sometimes even death.

What influence corruption had on the conduct and outcome of the Great Train Robbery I do not know. What is important, however, is when we interpret known facts about that case, we keep an open mind as to who might have benefitted from the truth being told or hidden and what secret motivations might have been at work.

I am not concerned here with the clear case that Goody had false forensic evidence given against him (police corruption) or that individuals were given 'verbals' (police corruption) because neither matter goes to the deeper underlying corruption. I believe police corruption had a bearing on the Great Train Robbery in at least two ways: firstly, I believe a corrupt transport detective might have assisted the robbers and I will discuss that in detail later in the book; secondly, I believe police corruption of a different sort might have impacted on identifying the mastermind.

The Flying Squad had a well-deserved reputation for achieving results. Putting aside the question of how those results were sometimes achieved, one practice that is not commonly known about is pertinent. The Flying Squad (they were not alone in this) would always want to be seen as having caught 'the big fish'. If there was a major crime case and the squad was perceived to have only caught the 'minnows', then their reputation would shrivel in the eyes of the press and the public. It would also be reduced in the eyes of villains too, and that matters. A criminal being interviewed, made false promises to, and assured by a member of an elite police squad, capable of granting freedom or a long prison sentence, would take the officer seriously.

However, if the Flying Squad's reputation were lessened, then operational deterioration would follow. And should the Flying Squad be seen to be incapable of catching a 'Mr Big', police bosses and their political masters would undoubtedly have replaced praise with criticism. Many generations ago, the police service found the answer: 'When you can't nick "Mr Big" then pretend "Mr Big" is one of those villains you have nicked.'

Imagine the lack of satisfaction that would have been felt by the Home Secretary if the Met Commissioner had to report that the squad had arrested all those Great Train Robbers who had attended the scene on the night but had been unable to identify the mastermind or the person who gave the inside information (they were, of course, two different people).

Detective Superintendent Butler, head of the Flying Squad, resolutely stood by his opinion that there was no mastermind. He was happy for Reynolds to be regarded as the ringleader. After all, not only was Reynolds in custody and pleading guilty he had been talking himself up for years. The head of the Flying Squad also said he saw no reason to conclude that there was any Post Office (or other) insider. Yet anyone who knows about the robbery surely has to conclude the very opposite about Reynolds' role, the mastermind and the insider.

SEVEN

MEETING TOM WISBEY AGAIN

Following the 'Gentry & Others' case in 1982, I rushed on with my life. The day after the trial I completed the necessary paperwork and put the case behind me. I had plenty of other cases on the go and new ones coming in regularly. At the time of the Gentry trial I had thirty-five professional mailbag thieves awaiting trial.

One of those cases involved a young man – memory tells me he was about 19. It was late one evening that I got a call from the Flying Squad at Kilburn. They had arrested young Joe McQuade on an unconnected matter and under questioning he had spoken about his knowledge of a £600,000 theft of mail from a train en route from Cambuslang. The squad wanted to know if I was aware of the crime and if I was already investigating it. I didn't even know where Cambuslang was, but rightly or wrongly professional pride led me to say, 'Yeah, I know all about it, I'll be straight over.' It took me a minute to find out that Cambuslang is cheek by jowl with Glasgow. It took me a few minutes more to find out the basic details of the crime.

When I arrived at Kilburn Police Station, the squad handed Joe and the Cambuslang investigation over to me, albeit reluctantly (but that's a whole different story). Joe gave me the names of the people who were involved. I phoned the Scottish Crime Squad and was fortunate enough to make contact with a DI Wilson. I told him my information and he warned me, 'Be careful Graham, we are talking about the worst mob in Glasgow. These people are capable of anything.'

Joe asked for bail and was granted it. The condition of bail was that he reported weekly in the early evening to Willesden Police Station. I carried on with the investigation, but I had so much on that the case was reallocated to a good friend of mine who shared the same office, DI Jim Walton. Three weeks later I received a phone call at home. Young Joe, as he left Willesden Police Station having reported as per his bail, had been shot through the eye, executed outside the police station.

There are several reasons for telling you that story. First and foremost it is to show how the organised theft of mailbags was not restricted to the London area. By 1981 there were definite and provable connections between mailbag thieves in Glasgow and London. The questions arising in other chapters are: When was that link forged, and was it prior to, and necessary to, the GTR?

As a matter of interest, some months later I had a phone call from the Scottish DI Wilson telling me they had arrested Joe's killer. He had been sent down from Glasgow to do the job. But the identity of those who paid for the hit, whilst known, could never be proven in court. No one would dare give evidence against them. Meanwhile, a Thames Valley detective inspector was investigating the circumstances that led to the mailbag thief known as Mousey MulCurran dying on the railway lines near Didcot. The officer was subjected to threats and an acid-throwing incident that resulted (thankfully) in damage only to his car.

On a different case I took a team to Manchester to investigate a big mailbag job there. We had information that the most well-known Manchester gang called 'The Quality Street Gang' had committed it. It was an awful experience; the smell of police corruption was thick in the air (I won't say more).

However, within two years I completed a Command Course at the Police Staff College in Hampshire and was awarded a scholarship to university. CID was put behind me for a while. Three years later, I returned to the force and was given a uniform inspector's job in the centre of that part of London with the highest crime rate: King's Cross.

There, I set up a charity to save Britain's earliest (*c.* 1862) public gymnasium that had been rotting and ignored for over seventy years. As a result, and with terrific good fortune, I met a man called Peter Kent. Peter was 63 at the time and had spent a lifetime in boxing. He was looking for a new home for the famous Gainsford Boxing club. He told me that the Gainsford's long lease on its old premises had expired with no (affordable) chance of it being renewed. The club was homeless. I could see how my gym, once refurbished and saved from redevelopment, might provide the Gainsford with a new home. I put that option to Peter and he could not have been more pleased (or relieved).

Peter and I became friends. He was a working-class bloke too and had spent all his life in inner-city London rubbing shoulders with the boxing fraternity. Did it ever occur to me that he might know a little about villains and villainy? Yes, of course. Did I ever find out if he had any 'form' or dodgy associates? No. Our friendship was based on creating, organising and managing boxing facilities for the railway men, local youth and transport policemen of King's Cross (as well as old Gainsford Club members). Little did I realise at the time the significance that Peter would have in events over twenty-five years later.

The gym was a great success; amateurs trained in the mornings, and in the afternoons and evenings we had top professional fighters. But it wasn't long before I moved on from King's Cross (promotion – still in uniform) and left the running of the gym to others. About every six months or so, Peter and I met for lunch.

It wasn't until about 2014 that the nature of our six-monthly lunch conversations changed. Peter invited me to join him and a friend at a 'knees-up' that was held regularly on a Sunday at his local pub. I showed a little polite interest and before I knew it Peter had me virtually committed to going. Then he hesitatingly explained that given my background, I might be a little reluctant to join the company of his pal, who, he said, had 'been a bit naughty in the past'. Of course, I pressed him on the issue, and he told me that the friend was Tom Wisbey. He asked me if I had ever heard of him.

Since that time, I've come to understand much better the link between Peter and Tom. Peter is clearly a man of considerable discretion, but I have since found out that he might be related by marriage to the Wisbey family. In addition, Peter had many years before worked 'in the print' with Tom's brothers. Clearly, there was a long-standing and trusted relationship between them.

No doubt Peter would have told Tom about how he and I created that successful gymnasium, about my lack of concern for any personal gain from it, and our (by then) long-term friendship. No doubt Tom reflected on the fact that in my past dealings with him I had been 'straight', with no hints of 'fit ups' or exaggeration of the evidence, and my rebuffing of a potential bribe to secure his release on bail.

But Tom Wisbey was a professional criminal. The record shows repeated convictions for very serious crimes. In addition, from the stories I have heard from more than one source, and the part stories Tom told me himself, he got away with more than he was captured for. And Tom Wisbey had not put crime or the accompanying 'macho' culture behind him. I have it on reliable word from a friend of Tom's named Malcolm Molyneux, that during Tom's last imprisonment, when he was in his late fifties, a tough guy in his thirties was determined to show to the other inmates that he was tougher than the infamous Tommy.

I am sure that Tom at that stage of his life would not have wanted to get involved in a tear-up. In the end the younger man attacked Tom and he had to defend himself. He beat the younger man severely enough for a lesson to have been learned. And of course Tom's record, by the year 2014, was not restricted to those crimes he committed prior to the Great Train Robbery or handling part of the considerable proceeds of Gentry & Others. It also included a long spell of imprisonment in connection with the supply of class-A drugs. Clearly, crime was not something that this man had got over, or grown away from.

I had reason to want to see Tom again: I wanted his help. But not so strongly as to be willing to give up time at the weekend to take part in a knees-up! The weekend is now family time. However, it wasn't long before we met. The first meeting took place in the Hilton Hotel in Park Lane. Peter and another friend of ours called Des were also present. The location, which was much more expensive than our usual haunts, had been chosen by Des. Over lunch I told Tom that I was writing a book about the train robbery. He listened intently. When I had finished, to my utter surprise, he offered to help.

It was easy company and a pleasant lunch (though slightly spoiled by the fact that it was Des's turn to pay and he skipped out early with a smile on his face!). We moved on to a bar (where, as always, I drank tea) and talked for another couple of hours. We met repeatedly thereafter and in the summer of 2015 he travelled down by train to see me. I picked him up at Grateley Station and took him to nearby Stockbridge where he stayed at The Grosvenor Hotel. He stayed for two or three nights and we met every day. We would work in his room, or in the bar, or across the road at Lilly Langtry's cafe.

It was a warm few days and we sat outside the cafe. He was amused at the idea of being in Stockbridge and thought it was fitting. I had no idea why. He told me that it was a haunt of Billy Hill, once the most powerful gangster in Britain and a significant character in the Great Train Robbery (I believe). That seemed unlikely. But he explained that Billy had a long-standing and well-known affair with Norah (Lady Docker). Lady Docker was an extremely glamorous socialite who often appeared in the pages of the popular press during the late '50s and early '60s. She was five years his senior.

She and her husband had a 170-acre estate nearby and Billy would come to Stockbridge to meet her. If you care to do a quick Google search, you will still find plenty of evidence to suggest such a relationship, as well as Billy's connection to Lady Docker's influential husband. You might also find a photograph taken of the two of them together at Gennaro's restaurant in Soho on the occasion of the launch of Billy's autobiography in 1953 (the year after the Eastcastle Street job – more on that later).

By the time Tom got on the train from Grateley back to Waterloo, I had a few scribbled notes and lots in my head. Tom and I met again, and he invited me to Joe Allen's restaurant near Covent Garden. We met again and again, and he remained happy to help.

The gangster Billy Hill with Lady Docker, as Lord Docker looks on.

In his autobiography, Bruce Reynolds claimed to be the leader of the GTR gang and lampooned Tom Wisbey by virtually saying his part was just to act as a 'donkey'. But Tom refused to criticise Reynolds in return. All he would say on the matter was, 'If anyone has the right to say they led the job on the ground it was Gordon (Goody).' But when it came to the Krays the antipathy was stronger. Once again, there were no actual insults, just a bland dismissiveness of their worth.

During that period of discussion between us, I suggested to him that it might be good to involve the only other living train robber, Bobby Welch. By the time Tom joined the gang, Bob Welch was already an experienced member. You might reasonably expect that Tom and he, having so much in common, might meet occasionally in their later lives to socialise. But Tom, who was known to be a social person, told me that he didn't see Bob anymore and mumbled something about him turning a bit 'funny' since he lost the use of one of his legs. I took him to mean that he had become difficult.

Tom on another occasion told me how disgracefully the Home Office had treated him. Whilst Tom was in prison, his teenage daughter, Lorraine, died suddenly in a car crash and the Home Office refused permission for him to attend the funeral. He was rightly bitter.

We spoke about other things too. He told me how following his last long prison sentence (for supplying a class-A drug) he had emigrated to the USA. No doubt minus a green card, he worked on a road-surfacing gang laying asphalt. He must have been in his sixties, and I admired the honesty of the labour. The story was slightly tarnished for me when he explained that once local hoods found out who he was, they were keen to be associated. Soon he was an enforcer again. He told me how easy the money was for the work he was given.

He described going to American nightclubs, the American villains he got tangled up with, and the international showbiz celebrities he was introduced to. He spoke about his family, about supporting Millwall Football Club as a child and then Arsenal. He spoke about Frank Sinatra, and a hundred other things. It is popularly written that he had a good singing voice, which he supposedly exercised at every opportunity. Tom told me that was all crap. He said his voice was nothing special at all. He just liked a sing-a-long.

But of course, Tom never let his guard down completely. I was never sure whether one or two revelations he shared were little 'testers' to see how I would respond. If he had confessed to any recent crime, it would have put me in a difficult position, but I would have been surprised if he had been foolish enough to put himself at risk in that way.

He was obviously still moving amongst senior crime figures in London. You probably remember the massive Hatton Garden Safe Deposit job. It took place one weekend in April 2015: goods to the value of £14 million or more were stolen. Remember all those old geezers being arrested with their pension books and National Health prescriptions visible in the back pocket of their M&S denims?

Well, I met Tom a few days after that crime. *The Times* was carrying a story that day that German lager tins had been left behind by the thieves. The journalist had put together a theory that the thieves might be German. We were discussing the case as we strolled through the City, then I said to him, 'Apparently the team might be German. They left German beer cans behind.' I didn't say it in order to judge his reaction, in order to 'get anything'; we were just making conversation. But I could tell by the slight pause in his response, the tone of his reply, that he knew much more. I left it at that.

Some people have asked me, 'why did he talk to *you*?' The simple answer is, I don't know. Maybe it was because he had just written his own book, *The Wrong Side of the Tracks*. That book tells his life story and includes an account of the Great Train Robbery and key events right up to Tom's late sixties.

Perhaps the completion of that book encouraged him to get involved in more of the same. He was certainly keen on the idea of writing more with me. He even suggested a plot on the lines of the well-known film, *Heat*. We joked about it, but I could tell he was really interested. He even said that if we ever did get such a film script written and made, that his part had to be played by Robert De Niro.

Why did he trust me? Perhaps because he had just lost the love of his life, his wife Renee, and felt he needed a distraction, I don't know. Was he helping me with the story because he wanted to earn money from it? I don't think so. He had been through the considerable effort of writing his memoir and travelled the country to promote it. He had made little from it. Very few people make any money from writing. What is more, and I know the following sounds unlikely and cynics will smirk and shake their heads, but nevertheless, Tom Wisbey told me that he couldn't make any money from helping me because he wasn't allowed to.

For the cynical, let me say that Tom paid for every aspect of his stay in Stockbridge and insisted on paying for the meal he bought me at Joe Allen's. Otherwise it was always strictly 50-50 – such as at our first meeting when Des scarpered without paying. He explained the authorities had made it plain they would jump all over him if he tried to make money out of the GTR. You might see inconsistencies in Tom's statements, but I can only tell you what I know.

Now, just to feed the cynics a few more crumbs ... I told him not to worry about potential income, or lack of it, that somehow I would make sure that he got a share of anything I might ever make. But can you see the subtle difference? He came to the table saying, 'I will help you without promise of personal gain.'

I guess that last remark sort of refers back to the question, 'Why would he tell *you*?' He could certainly have taken his secrets to any journalist. So the bottom line is, I don't really know, but trust was involved.

Of course what I wanted was the full inside story, all the stuff that had never been revealed before: the unidentified robbers, the identity of Mr Big, the truth about the insider, where all the money went and so on. But Tom was no grass. There really were some old-time villains who enjoyed the reputation of keeping their mouths closed, admitting nothing and implicating no one. It was not honour amongst thieves. There is no such thing.

In 1981/82, a supergrass (as they were known) called John Moriarty (who I will tell you more about later) was being held in Reading Prison where I visited him regularly. He told me how he and Tom Wisbey had planned the following: Tom arranged to pay a big amount of money for a substantial consignment of cannabis. At the exchange, pot for cash, after Tom had inspected the goods and was in the process of handing over a briefcase of money, the drug dealer and he were surprised by the arrival of CID officers.

Tom and the drug dealer were both 'arrested'. They were put into separate vehicles and driven away. The drug dealer was driven to the local police station where the 'CID' vehicle parked outside. The two 'officers' told their prisoner to stay in the back of the car and that they would be back in '30 seconds'. Both 'CID' men went into the police station (where they simply asked for directions to some place or other). Two minutes later they returned to their car to find the 'prisoner' had escaped. The two men drove off to meet Tom, mission nicely accomplished. Tom paid John Moriarty and his fellow CID impersonator handsomely.

When I asked Tom about it he said he didn't remember it at all!

Anyway, Tom's refusal to identify a suspect in any crime was not because he had any great affection for the thousands of people who fill jail cells, or should do. It was not honour amongst thieves but something more. A professional villain cannot succeed if he is known to be an informer. No one wants a grass on the firm. Becoming known as, or suspected of being, an informer puts the individual at the mercy of both villains and unscrupulous police officers. It is simply not a good career move. Once labelled an informer, any spell of imprisonment becomes a nightmare and special protective measures have to be taken, which result in even greater social isolation. Furthermore, after a lifetime of being a respected face, Tom would certainly not be prepared to throw away a hard-won reputation.

So, I had to think creatively. I suggested to him that we 'write a novel'. It would be a story about the GTR that actually revealed the truth. I could write a letter on his behalf explaining to anyone that cared to enquire (such as any over-enthusiastic detective) that he and I were just writing a story of pure fiction (see Appendix 2). By this means he could tell me the truth. As we both knew, the story about the GTR would also be a story about crimes that he and others had never been charged with. Theoretically, he could still have been answerable in law to such charges.

Tom warmed to the plan and agreed to the idea and we got on with the story. But where fact ended and fiction started was not always easy to tell. I noticed that his comments, remarks and contributions were of three types. Some things he would freely contribute and embellish if encouraged. Some he would want to have time to reflect on before committing to, and there were a few occasions when I voiced a logical conclusion that he would shy away from. The last group includes his response to my conclusion that Billy Hill was behind the Great Train Robbery. After he had chewed it over he suggested we use another 'Billy'. Billy Howard was mentioned (another well-known and extremely violent contemporary of Billy Hill). I remember responding that

I didn't want any old 'Billy', I wanted the truth (in our work of fiction). He reluctantly agreed.

People have asked me since if I tape-recorded our conversations. Tom would have wondered what I was up to. People have asked if I took contemporaneous notes of our meetings. I have no doubt that it would have brought things to a halt. People have asked if I had my photograph taken with him. For Pete's sake …

When I got to the stage of nearing the completion of the first draft of the novel, I phoned Tom's number. His grandson answered it; he told me that Tom had suffered a stroke and had been hospitalised. I contacted Peter Kent and we went to visit Tom in University College Hospital. There I met Tom's daughter, Marilyn, for the first time. She was at his bedside constantly. Tom never recovered enough to read the draft novel, nor did I ever get the chance to ask him any of the many questions that remained unanswered. We simply ran out of time. Tom Wisbey's condition gradually deteriorated and he died in December 2016.

I have only told you a little about the insight I gained into Tom Wisbey's character. I learned much more than I can share with you here. In her book, Peta Fordham says, 'The criminal far more than the ordinary honest citizen, understands the meaning of good faith, though he may not practice it himself.'[*] I think Tom knew it when he saw it.

Tom was a violent and determined criminal, but he was not just that. He was also an ordinary man, modest, amusing, discreet and generous, and a father loved by his surviving daughter and grandson.

I saw Bob Welch at Tom's funeral. He was in a wheelchair and surrounded by a small group of much younger men. They were giggling and joking about something or other. During 2018, I managed to get a copy of the synopsis and notes on the novel I had written with Tom to Bob Welch. A little while later I spoke to him on the phone, or I tried to.

On one occasion when I was with Tom he told me this story about Bob Welch. The gang was hiding at some place in the

---

[*] Fordham, *The Robbers' Tale*, Preface.

countryside. They had been there long enough for Bob Welch to 'make friends' and gain the trust of a duck or goose (I can't remember which) that wandered around the place. The bird trusted him. One afternoon Bob and another of the gang left the hideout for a couple of hours. When Bob got back he found that one of the gang had strangled the bird and hung it up for Bob to find. Apparently, Bob went berserk.

So, I thought, somewhere in his personality there is something good, something I might reach out to. But when I spoke to him on the phone that day last year he made it abundantly clear that he was unhappy at the thought of what we had written.

EIGHT

MICHELANGELO OR MICKEY MOUSE?

Well, was Reynolds, 'Michelangelo' and the brains behind the robbery, the leader of the pack as most people now think? Was he an artist? Was the Great Train Robbery his 'Sistine Chapel' as he claimed? Or was he a 'Mickey Mouse' character, and little more than a cynical 'brand' developed by his inflated ego and a few sycophants?

I can tell you with absolute conviction: he was neither. Two questions are addressed in this chapter: firstly, was Reynolds an artist, a highly sensitive, intelligent person, an intellectual even? Secondly, was he the leader of the GTR gang?

After his death, the *Independent*, reporting on his funeral, tore into the memory of Reynolds with very harsh words:

These men (train robbers) were the Raoul Moats or Dale Cregans of a bygone era. It is just that the passing of the years softens and sentimentalises the public view. So much so that the media was straight-facedly reporting Ronnie Biggs' son paying tribute to Reynolds as 'a very, very kind person who was a true gentleman who made many friends in his life'. Yes and Hitler was a vegetarian who loved cream cakes and banned cruelty to lobsters. The truth about Bruce Reynolds was that he was a low-life loser who came out of jail after

Britain's greatest robbery and was back behind bars a few years
later for peddling amphetamines.[*]

The article had not a single positive, or even neutral, statement to make about Reynolds. Surely, no one could write off
another human being so utterly, without having first studied
the evidence (and looked inwards at the dark corners of their
own personality)?

Having done my homework – looking at Reynolds' own
words and those of his associates, his record of behaviour (so far as
is possible) and at what the police knew of him – I can say with
certainty that he was not the person of popular myth.

Bruce Richard Reynolds was born at Charing Cross Hospital,
London, on 7 September 1931. The records show that his father
was a porter and his mother a nurse. They lived in a flat in Putney
before moving to Essex. Reynolds' mother died when he was still
a small boy, and this was followed shortly after by the death of his
sister. Before too long Reynolds' father started a new relationship
and Reynolds moved in with his grandmother. It seems that it
was at this stage that things started to go wrong.

Reynolds' descent into crime started when he masterminded
the bold if somewhat foolish crime of … riding a bike without
lights. Thereafter, as a teenager he began his life of theft rather
modestly. Eventually he was sentenced to borstal training. After
release, he fell back into the easiest way to make a living – taking
other people's hard-earned cash. In 1957 Reynolds (with long-
time friend Terry Hogan) robbed a bookmaker and inflicted
grievous bodily harm on his victim. That year he also stabbed two
uniformed constables. He was subsequently sentenced at the Old
Bailey, in January 1958, to two and a half years' imprisonment for
wounding with intent. So much for his aversion to violence.

But was he an intellectual artist? Remember, it was Reynolds
who described the Great Train Robbery as his 'Sistine Chapel'.
Of course, you might think that, by definition, being an armed
robber and man of violence would automatically preclude him

---

[*] Paul Varley, *The Independent,* 28 March 2013.

from being an artist and intellectual. There seems to be several generations of people who are prepared to accept his personal view of himself at face value, yet the evidence shows no artistic achievement. Nor does it show that he ever spent any time studying any aspect of art or creativity. All we have are his claims and a little name-dropping.

I think the rot started when Ronnie Biggs described Reynolds to the writer Peta Fordham. That description of Reynolds' character has taken root, grown and flourished. I must say her descriptions of each of the robbers is remarkable; she appears one of many to see them as modern 'Merry Outlaws of Nottingham Forest'. This is part of her description of Biggs and his relationship with Reynolds:

> Biggs, whose large, vacant, pale blue eyes seem at variance with the rest of an intelligent, kindly face, worked tirelessly on (at the robbery). I can picture him as the 'Boxer' of the enterprise, that large, loyal, not very bright, carthorse of Orwells' 1984 [sic] … He was with his hero, Reynolds and, like any other schoolboy worshipper of a cricket captain, was happy to fag for his god.**

So where can we find any expression of Reynolds the artist? He did write a memoir of course, *The Autobiography of a Thief*, and it galls me to say it, but I think it's quite interesting. In my humble opinion, however, it shows no intellectual strength, no self-awareness, no meaningful reflection, no philosophical expression and no observation on the human condition. So, I see no evidence of any artistic creation by Reynolds, other than his own viewing of the GTR as some sort of performance art.

I am reliably informed that Reynolds wrote 'one or two articles' for *The Guardian* newspaper. Unfortunately I have not been able to find them, so I can't comment. It is certainly true to say that many aspiring writers who have tried to get something published in that newspaper have failed (I'm one of them).

** Fordham, *The Robbers' Tale*, p.71.

Apparently, Reynolds used to send his *Guardian* writing fees to Amnesty International. I've never done that either.

Of course, any intellectual who is reading this (an unlikely event) might want to point out that 'there is no such thing as art, only artists'. I have always taken that statement to mean that a person who 'sees' art of whatever type is therefore an artist. It follows that art is whatever such a person perceives it to be. I must concede, on this understanding of art, Reynolds might have been Michelangelo, albeit one who never produced any actual art. But, by the same measure, so might all the other train robbers and my Aunt Sally too.

But perhaps I'm being unfair; perhaps Reynolds' whole life was 'performance art' and not just the train robbery. How would we expect such a life to be lived? We know something about the way that Gandhi lived his life in furtherance of his art (of moral and political philosophy). He might be an extreme example, but you see my point.

Reynolds, like one or two more of those involved, did not stand trial at the same time as the bulk of the others. He managed to evade arrest for some months. But I have seen no evidence that he was judged to be the leader of the gang by those who heard the facts of the case against him at the time. At the time of Reynolds' trial, an innocent man, called Boal, had been found guilty of the robbery and sentenced to twenty-five years' imprisonment. Reynolds, unlike the vast majority, pleaded guilty.

In pleading guilty, Reynolds would have had nothing to lose by telling the truth about Boal. Boal had played no part in the planning or execution of the robbery and Reynolds knew that and kept quiet.

Reynolds, the self-proclaimed boss, philosopher, artist and romantic, did not take the opportunity to see that wrong righted. Instead, like the others, he stood by whilst Boal suffered and died in prison for a crime he did not commit. It was not until many years had gone by, and long after Boal had fought hard to clear his name and died in prison, that Reynolds eventually spoke up.

Years after the GTR, Reynolds' long-time buddy Terry Hogan's stated belief was that it was Reynolds who coshed Driver Mills.

That may or may not have been the case, but it indicates the view of Reynolds' character by a close associate: Reynolds had a ready willingness to inflict violence.

I am not saying that 'an artist' cannot be violent; I am not saying that 'an intellectual' cannot lose his temper. But I am saying that no such person can live a life that consists of regularly planning and using dishonesty and violence against innocent victims without actually expressing some tangible form of artistic or intellectual quality in support of his claim.

I do not doubt for one minute that Bruce Reynolds very much desired to be viewed as a well-read, creative intellectual. I think that by the end of this chapter you will at least suspect that he was prone to fantasy and self-delusion. I learned a long time ago that the best liars are those who convince themselves that they are telling the truth. They lie to themselves.

From reading *The Robbers' Tale*, it is clear that the author admires Reynolds' charm, but even she says of Reynolds in his youth:

> the streak of violence that lies in him began to come out, his obvious attraction for women began to bring its own complications. He became aggressively possessive … If he took a woman out two or three times she was his. 'She dared not look at another fellow' one friend said. He was likely to go for the other chap and beat him up.*

Apparently, during one spell of imprisonment, Reynolds heard that an ex-girlfriend was seeing one of his former gang of thieves. It seems Reynolds got himself stabbed in order to more easily get out of prison and seek revenge. Does this sound like a man of sensitivity? A man with any awareness of the human condition? Does it sound like an artist?

So, if he was not an artist, did he at least provide the leadership for the planning and execution of the GTR? Upon completion

---

* Fordham, *The Robbers' Tale*, p.153.

of the main trial, the judge addressed the prisoners. This is what he said before sentencing one of them:

> You have manifest gifts of personality and intelligence which might have carried you far had they been directed to honesty … I have not seen you in court for the best of three months without noticing signs that you are a man capable of inspiring the admiration of your fellow accused. In the Army you earned a very good character assessment and it is easy to imagine you becoming, in an entirely honourable role, a leader of your comrades, but you have become a dangerous menace to society. *

Question. Who was the judge addressing? Bruce Reynolds? Well, no actually, he was describing Gordon Goody. Tom Wisbey confirmed to me that if there was a leader on the ground, it was Gordon Goody.

In his book, *How to Rob a Train*, Goody talks at length about Reynolds. He starts this way:

> Let me make one thing perfectly clear from the start. Bruce Reynolds has been a very close personal friend of mine for most of our lives and remained so until his death in February 2013, (But) I do take exception to being referred to, as I have been from time to time, as Bruce's number two. I wasn't number two to anybody. **

Because, with the passing of time, 'second in command' is the role that Reynolds tried to impose on his old friend. Goody continues:

> Bruce freely admitted that he craved peer recognition … He liked to cast himself in the role of a Raffles-type gentleman

---

* Lord Edmund Davies' pre-sentencing address, 15 April 1964, Aylesbury court.
** Gordon Goody, *How to Rob a Train*, location 42.

burglar and he wanted to be able to walk into a pub and have people mutter, 'That's Bruce Reynolds, the master criminal.'***

Reynolds tells us in his memoir that he was known by the GTR gang as the 'Major'. Leaving aside that the police only found one officer's uniform at Leatherslade, that of a lieutenant, when I put Reynolds' claim to Tom Wisbey, he just smiled thinly. If Tom didn't exactly shake his head at the same time, then the smile did it for him. Gordon Goody had no such reservations: 'Bruce, "The Schoolmaster" we used to call him.'**** No one other than Reynolds himself seems to have called him the 'Major'.

But those opinions aside, it is quite possible to reach our own conclusions by looking at the available evidence. It was Reynolds who introduced Biggs. Biggs was a professional failure, from commencing a career criminal's life by being caught stealing pencils, right up to his penultimate conviction for stealing a bike. During that period he was variously caught for theft, burglary and housebreaking but found time to set up and fail as a self-employed builder.

However, there are two things that Biggs did very well after achieving infamy. Firstly, he pumped up the considerable ego of his old mate Bruce by describing him as the 'brains' and the 'leader' of the train robbery gang. And secondly, he took on the mantle of cunning criminal fox, outsmarting the best that NSY could offer. The fact that Biggs lived a life out of reach of the British courts says more about lack of international agreement than it does Biggs' cleverness.

I suspect that Biggs might have been so ill-informed, and so kept at bay by the other robbers, that he did indeed think his chum Bruce, who know doubt gave *him* his instructions, was the boss. It is generally accepted that the rest of the gang thought 'Bigsy' wasn't up to scratch, and you can imagine they would not want any more to do with him than necessary. Goody is on record as saying that Biggs wasn't a train robber at all; he was just invited along.

***   Goody, *How to Rob a Train*, location 50.
****   Goody, *How to Rob a Train*, p.93.

Secondly, it was, of course, Reynolds who was at the centre of events in the purchasing of Leatherslade Farm. It was Reynolds who visited in person the estate agent and opened the discussion on its purchase. It really was a dumb move and was bound to lead back to the gang after the robbery.

As soon as the police found Leatherslade Farm scattered with empty mailbags and a mountain of evidence, they would naturally enquire of the owner. That would equally, of course, have been the case if, as planned, the farmhouse had been suspiciously burned down within 48 hours of the robbery. Police enquiries were bound (as they did) to lead straight back to the estate agent. And the police were certain to ask the estate agent for a description of the man who had shown the initial interest and opened up negotiations.

Any villain worth his salt would instead have made the enquiries at the estate agent by phone using a false name and an accommodation address. Then they would have opened a bank account using those details. In those days, pre money-laundering legislation, it really was that easy. Then, using those false particulars they would have purchased/leased Leatherslade Farm with no easy route for the police, or the estate agent, to identify them.

Thirdly, Reynolds claims to have chosen the location for the robbery, yet his technical knowledge of the railways was zero. That ignorance seems to have continued throughout his life. You might think that if he were going to make such a claim he would have first taken the time to find out what criteria might be used in making the selection. You might think he would bother to learn a bit about the need to understand the signalling system and how the train guard on the TPO would react to an unforeseen red light. As you will see later, he did none of these things. He simply never seemed to understand the vital importance of how to choose the right place and time to stop the train.

Fourthly, most people have accepted Reynolds' statement that on the night of the robbery, he dressed as a major before setting off from Leatherslade Farm for Bridego Bridge. Even though it was probably a lieutenant's garb, Goody's comment is worth considering: 'Bruce was wearing a paratrooper's smock and a beret with an SAS emblem affixed. I can't say for sure if there were officer's insignia attached but I'd be surprised if there weren't.'* In other words, Bruce liked to pretend.

So the notion that Reynolds creates in his biography that he strolled around Leatherslade Farm before the robbery in his major's outfit reassuring and motivating his 'troops' is silly. Goody would surely have remembered it.

Here is a short extract from Reynolds' autobiography:

> We changed into our uniforms and prepared ourselves. Hardly a word was spoken. I suddenly felt a great sense of affection for my troops. **

It sounds as if it has been lifted (stolen) from a Second World War adventure yarn, and it might well have been.

You would reasonably expect that each robber would know his own particular role and they would all leave Leatherslade Farm in their various vehicles according to their destination and job. This seems to have happened, with Reynolds (northern outpost) travelling with the 'signals team' – Daly and Cordrey – plus Ronnie Biggs and 'Stan' (or 'Pop' or 'Peter') – the replacement train driver.

Biggs would have waited with the replacement driver near the signals. Once called, he would bring the replacement driver to the locomotive. Those who had the job, once the train had stopped, of uncoupling the train and overpowering the driver and his assistant, would travel together to that location. Those who were going to smash their way in to the coaches at Bridego Bridge would travel together to Bridego Bridge. That's all pretty basic stuff, right?

But no, according to Reynolds his vehicle, with the 'signals team', first went to Bridego Bridge. He describes how once there, he climbed the embankment onto the railway and urinated:

---

*   Goody, *How to Rob a Train*.
** Reynolds, *The Autobiography of a Thief*, p.244.

It was more than just relief. Perhaps subconsciously I was establishing territorial boundaries like a tomcat or a lion. This is my domain.[*]

No, it wasn't. Though he seems to have believed it was.

He says that while surveying his domain and contemplating what was to follow, he lit a fine cigar:

I knew I would not have time to finish it, but a Montecristo No.2 is a fine companion to have whilst awaiting your destiny … This was … my Eldorado. Visions of Drake and his motley crew at Panama.[**]

There must surely be every reason to conclude that the robbers would have gone straight to their respective areas of business. Would they all simply congregate together on the busiest of the quite roads in the area in order that Bruce might dream of being Lawrence of Arabia (or whatever) whilst he took a leak?

Sixthly, we know Roger Cordrey was well versed in stopping trains at the right spot without raising an alarm. Yet his instructions as to how to change the dwarf signal (while he worked on the overhead signals mounted on the gantry) were ignored. This could have completely ruined their plans. The way the signal was interfered with caused a warning to flash in the signal box. Who was responsible? We know by his own admission that Reynolds was there or nearby. We know his brother-in-law John Daly was too. So, was it his brother-in-law or Reynolds? We will never know. But we do know that if Reynolds was not personally responsible but simply present or nearby, he showed a remarkable lack of understanding, and/or lack of leadership.

We also know that Reynolds went straight from the signals to his lookout post. There he awaited first signs of the TPO. As soon as he saw or heard or felt it coming he radioed his accomplices and headed for Bridego Bridge, only stopping momentarily to

---

[*] Reynolds, *The Autobiography of a Thief*, p.240.

[**] Reynolds, *The Autobiography of a Thief*.

pick up his accomplice Daly. This is the accepted version. But Reynolds in his autobiography adds that before he left the look-out position, he placed detonators on the track in accordance with BR regulations in order to prevent an accident.*** Strange that, because to walk a mile north and a mile south (as per those regulations) plus the mile back to his car would have taken him at least forty-five minutes, and the 'leader' would have missed the robbery completely.

But more than that, if he walked the track to lay detonators as he alleges, it was a miracle that he didn't bump into the guard from the train they had just forced to stop. It seems that both men were putting detonators down at the same time on the same track. Perhaps they exchanged pleasantries, Bruce, having walked north and placed his detonators, being on his way back south to his car, and the guard, heading north to do likewise. You can imagine it: 'Evening Lieutenant err … sorry, Major.' 'Good evening, my man, what a beautiful summer's night. Would you like a cigar?'

It's all too daft for words. Reynolds is lying again. But the lies are not the lies of a clever man. They are so easily identified by anyone who takes care to look at the facts.

So why does Bruce Reynolds deceive us by saying he laid detonators? I can only think it is a misguided answer to those who have criticised the robbers for stopping a train in a way that could have led to disaster. For if another train had been following on the same fast line a few minutes behind the TPO, and the red lights had not been indicated in the signal box (and because of Cordrey's method, they would not have been), then this was a distinct possibility. It is another crude attempt to manage Reynolds' public image.

It was a strict rule that when a train made an unscheduled stop (other than in a station) for any emergency, the guard of the train would have to attach detonators to the running lines (rails) at regular intervals behind and in front of the train for a distance of a mile. Then in the event of a train approaching the

***   Reynolds, *The Autobiography of a Thief*, p.247.

stationary one, the approaching train driver would be alerted by the sound of the detonations.

Every gang of labourers has to have a ganger as well as a boss. As I will show later, the boss was Hill and his managers were the Krays, but who was the ganger on site?

As I said earlier, Lord Edmund Davies, having heard all the evidence, identified Goody as the leader of the gang. Fordham has no doubts about Goody: 'Goody was in command at Leatherslade: he had them all on their toes'.[*]

Reynolds says, and it is uncontested, that his job that night was to tell the rest of the gang as soon as he was sure the train was coming. This is an important point. As Russell-Pavier/Richards point out:

> Although Reynolds looked the part of a commander in his fake major's uniform and SAS cap badge, there is a paradox about the <u>self-proclaimed leader</u> of the gang he later claimed to be, not engaged in the field of battle, not leading his men, <u>but voyeuristically observing them</u> and the jeopardy of others from a safe distance.[**]

And there you have it.

Of course, your work experience and your viewing of politicians might lead you to conclude that this sort of ducking away from the front line is absolutely typical of leadership. But when it comes to the sharp end – field activity in the armed services, competitive team sports, working on a building site, running your own business and so on, all effective leaders on the ground need to be visible, and visibly in charge, to have real authority. You do not do that by donning the right 'uniform' and hiding on the fringes. No gang member, other than Reynolds himself and his idiot associate, saw Reynolds as the leader.

Many of us remember from our school, or teenage years, when as part of a gang, we went scrumping apples or pinching a Kit-Kat

---

[*] Fordham, *The Robbers' Tale*, p.59.

[**] Russell-Pavier/Richards, *Crime of the Century*, p.26.

from Woolworths. But where did the ringleader stand, near the garden fence to watch out for the apple tree owner? Near the shop door ready to call you if staff seemed to have become suspicious at the bigger boys' interest in the chocolate bars? No. Those lookout jobs were left to the boy who could easily be persuaded that he sounded like Elvis. That night on the railway, Reynolds followed orders; he was told to go as far north as possible and let the others know when the train was coming. That's it.

Within one week of the GTR the Flying Squad had the names of key suspects – John Daly, Gordon Goody, Roy James, Bruce Reynolds, Charlie Wilson. Two observations are worth making. Firstly, these men are all part of the supposed 'Reynolds (Goody's) gang'. If he was their leader, then his leadership had led them to detection pretty smartly. Conversely, none of the South Coast Raiders gang was initially named. Clearly, they had taken rather better precautions, though their names followed within days.

The first member of the South Coast Raiders to appear on a suspects' list was Bob Welch. He was the only one who had been identified some time earlier as involved with Goody's gang in the acquisition of Post Office uniforms, allegedly something to do with an intended attack on a Southern Region train.

The robbers had apparently paid for any potential forensic evidence at their hideout (Leatherslade Farm) to be thoroughly destroyed once they had vacated. The clean-up simply was not done, and the result was a mountain of scientific evidence just waiting for the police to find. Who was it that arranged for this work to be done? According to the Metropolitan Police it was a William Still, a close associate of Bruce Reynolds!

Three weeks after the GTR, Commander Hatherill, the senior-most Metropolitan Police officer actively engaged on the case, held a meeting with the Deputy Controller of the Post Office Investigation Department and other senior representatives of the agencies involved. Hatherill had reason to believe that the loot had been divided into eighteen lots, one for each of the fourteen offenders that were on his suspects' list, one for each of the two alleged Post Office insiders, one for the man who had bought Leatherslade farm and *one for the organiser*. Note, Reynolds was on

Hatherill's list that day as one of the robbers, and the organiser remained unidentified. Thus Reynolds was definitely not considered by Hatherall to be the organiser or mastermind.

Having said all that, I am sure that during the time that the Goody team operated prior to the involvement of the South Coast Raiders, Reynolds played a significant part in the Goody team. But there can be no doubt, that once the self-promotion of Reynolds is removed, and the words of those who knew the individuals are studied, and the views of those who saw the trial play out are considered, that Goody led the team on the day. As I said before, Tom told me, 'If anyone had a right to claim leadership at the robbery it was Gordon (Goody).'

Since the robbery in 1963, there has been a growing belief that the train robbers were folk heroes. That falsity might have started within days of the trial, but by the end of it, a romanticised version of a violent crime perpetuated by violent and determined men had certainly been born. And if I have one significant criticism of the very warm and thoughtful book that Peta Fordham published shortly after the trial, it is the romanticisation of violent criminals.

According to her account, all of the robbers are likeable rogues: 'Buster is a genial character ... kindly ... one of the keenest brains'.* Of Gordon Goody (violent robber) she says: 'A man of cold courage and sardonic humour, a more than life-sized figure, with nerves of steel and the wolfish handsomeness of the pack leader, that in fact he is'.**

So is there anything in Reynolds' childhood and teenage years to indicate that he had leadership qualities? As a boy he seems to have had a bit of a rough time. When I read about his childhood it reminded me of my own: air weapons, council estate, great sadness, loneliness, a little minor lawbreaking and fantasy. It also reminded me of a question I asked my sister just a few years ago: 'Marion, were we poor as kids?' She responded: 'No poorer than those around us.' It was the perfect answer. As a child, whether

---

* Fordham, *The Robbers' Tale*, p.33.

** Fordham, *The Robbers' Tale*, p.29.

your name is Reynolds or Patel, whether you frequent a palace or a council flat, whatever is around you is, by definition, normal. It is not, in itself, an excuse to turn against society.

As a child, to have immature ideas out of all proportion to the realities of the world is normal. But surely the usual growing awareness and development of 'self' and knowledge of the outer world means that by our mid-teens most of us have some idea who we are and how our personal ambitions measure against the actual world of opportunity. This stage of ordinary human development seems to have largely eluded Reynolds.

According to his biography, as an 18-year-old (and older) he thought he could walk into a journalist's job in Fleet Street, join a medical organisation and, in his words, 'change the world of medicine'. He thought he could join the armed services as an officer. He really seems to have thought he could do all, or any, of those things without any formal qualification and with a criminal record. This is surely a staggering state of mind for an 18-year-old. It is made all the queerer because he repeats it all in his biography with no sense of embarrassment, irony or mitigation.

Of course, being a fantasist does not mean that the sufferer is ineffective. What sort of weird fantasies must Hitler or Fred West have held? The world of fantasy, a life of fantasy, is not necessarily an innocent one. So, was he the mastermind and leader of the gang? No. And as for his being a 'Mickey Mouse' character, that is certainly not true either.

Reynolds may have played a significant part in the robbery (over and above what was accepted in evidence of his guilt), but it is not the one that he describes. Reynolds built a relationship with the man I believe to be the true mastermind, Billy Hill. Reynolds might well have been a conduit for Hill's inspiration and guidance to the team. To that extent he may have been instrumental.

Finally, during Reynolds' life there was much to disdain and in his character much to dislike. But there is at least one very important and good thing he left behind – love between father and son. This is part of what his son, Nick, said at his father's funeral:

(He was) my best friend, soul mate and older brother ... He chose a lunatic path and paid the price ... He was an artist at heart ... (but) his greatest triumph was in reassessing himself and changing his attitude about what was important in life.[*]

Finally, on the issue of Reynolds being the alleged mastermind, Fordham says of the months before the robbery:

The police, for their part, also knew that something was in the wind, but they had no idea what. One of the most mysterious things about the whole operation is the fact that no useful word of the secret reached the police in advance through any informer. That this is in some measure due to the respect with which the 'Mind' is regarded in the underworld is undoubted.

Does that sound like a description of Bruce Reynolds as he was known to the world in 1963? No.

There is one remote, reasonable and logical explanation as to why Bruce Reynolds might have been determined to inflate his own importance and his part in the planning and execution of the robbery: money. Most of the robbers ended their lives in rather poor circumstances; I have no reason to think otherwise of Reynolds. Recently, I found that during his more mature years he was autographing old ten-shilling and pound banknotes and offering them for sale as if they were part of the loot. Similarly, he had autographed other items including pieces of steel mounted like a trophy and said to be from the rail track where the robbery occurred. You can still see them on eBay. So, just perhaps, the self-promotion, the building of 'Brand Bruce' was just a way of raising the value of his products. If that were the case, and in private he had a more realistic sense of 'self', then sympathy would be appropriate.

---

[*] Duncan Campbell, *The Guardian*, 20 March 2013.

NINE

THE MASTERMIND AND HIS ENFORCERS

Lord Edmund Davies said at the conclusion of the main GTR trial: 'The Crown have said they do not consider this criminal enterprise was the product of any criminal mastermind. I do not know that I necessarily agree.' On that theme, Peta Fordham, who witnessed the trial, concluded, in support of the judge's opinion, that one of the most startling aspects of the whole business was the absolute silence that was maintained by the robbers throughout the whole proceedings including the period when several were 'on the run'.

You might reasonably ask, why? The answer is simple: 'threats and promises'. In his extremely well-researched book, Andrew Cook also makes the point that the key question of the identity of the person behind the GTR has remained a mystery.

I have already referred to the meeting that Commander Hatherill, head of New Scotland Yard's intelligence gathering department (C11), had three weeks after the robbery. Also present were the Deputy Controller of the Post Office Investigation Department and other senior representatives of the agencies involved in the case. Hatherill had reason to believe the loot had been divided into eighteen lots. By the time of that meeting the names of the fourteen suspects were pretty accurate:

1. Goody
2. Wilson
3. Reynolds

4. White
5. Smith
6. James
7. Daly
8. Edwards
9. Wisbey
10. Pembroke
11. Hussey
12. Cordrey
13. Welch

All of the above were suspected to have been at the scene and actively engaged in the robbery, but added to that list was:

14. Brian Field: the man who organised the purchase of Leatherslade Farm for use by the robbers.

Note the absence of Biggs. He was, of course, not regarded as a 'serious villain' and his name therefore would not have quickly surfaced via informants, or as a result of his petty crime record. Unlike the others, Biggs did not have a file at C11; that department would never have heard of him.

If all the main conspirators each had a fair share of the proceeds, which they would have of course, then the amount that each received is the key to the total number of robbers involved. While each robber would be entitled to a 'whack' (equal percentage), others on the periphery would get a 'drink' (a small payment).

With the passage of time, if we take the conclusions of the criminal trials and the considerable analysis that has been done by many over the fifty years since, plus the revelations made by Tom Wisbey, the true list of robbers looks like this:

1. Goody
2. Wilson
3. Reynolds
4. White
5. James
6. Danny Pembroke (see Chapter 15)

7. Daly – he was acquitted but was in reality a full participant.
8. Edwards
9. Wisbey
10. Hussey
11. Cordrey
12. Welch
13. Freddie Sansom (see Chapter 15)
14. Biggs

All of the above were at the scene but then we add:

15. Brian Field
16. The Mastermind
17. The Krays or other enforcers
18. The Insider(s)

Goody also says the money was divided into eighteen shares of £150,000. But that would amount to a total sum of £2,700,000. The total stolen was just over £2,600,000.

In addition, £150k per person would allow nothing for others who would have undoubtedly assisted the robbers and been paid a 'drink'.

More reliable, but more confusing, was the scribbled note found in Roy James' possession after arrest. It was apparently screwed up in the corner of a holdall. Perhaps each of the robbers had been given these calculations that resulted in the amount they received, who knows? But the note, which was produced in evidence and was not in James' handwriting, apparently read:[*]

1st, 22,500 = 5	*(= 112,500)*
2nd, 15,000 = 1	*(= 15,000)*
3rd, 18,200 = 1	*(= 18,000)*
4th, 6,800 = 1.5	*(= 10,200)*
5th 14,000 = 5	*(= 90,000)*
	(Total £245,700)
	(Above – my notes in brackets in this column)

[*] Fordham, *The Robbers' Tale*, p.111.

The note was alleged by the prosecution to represent some sort of calculation of share of the stolen money. I wish I had access to the mathematician who worked that out, because I simply cannot see it! (James was found with £109,500 in his possession.) Perhaps the sums represented the amount of money that James had counted from the mailbags during the 'count and divvy up'?

Roger Cordrey was found soon after the robbery and charged with receiving £141,000. This seems to me to be the best prediction of the share out. Eighteen multiplied by £141,000 equals £2,538,000. This leaves a remainder to be paid out as 'drinks' to those who assisted in lesser ways (e.g. buy the farm, burn the farm).

Incidentally, we hear various amounts quoted as representing the total haul. Anywhere between £2.4 million and £2.6 million plus. There may be a technical reason for this. We know that certain mailbags containing money were left behind on the TPO by the robbers having been 'taken' by them (as part of the entire load) on taking charge of the TPO and unlawfully moving it forward to Bridego Bridge. Technically therefore it is possible to say that legally they stole all of it, even though they abandoned some of it before making off to their hideout. Furthermore, at Bridego Bridge, where they unloaded and made off with as much as they could in the time allowed, they left at least one bag on the embankment. The same legal argument could be applied (stolen and abandoned).

All the evidence indicates that fewer than eighteen robbers were in attendance, perhaps as few as fourteen, and so the necessity for other equal shares indicate the involvement of an insider, a mastermind and another party.

I believe the mastermind was Billy Hill: the most powerful London-born international gangster of the time. Billy Hill was born in 1911, in the most violent, poverty stricken, criminal part of London, to a mother and father who were criminals. He was the youngest of numerous criminal siblings. They were not just a family of thieves; they were violent, persistent, small time, poverty stricken professionals. And when Billy stepped out from the thieves' den that he called home, he found himself in crowded streets filled with rather similar people.

Thieving and bullying by the time he could walk, at the age of 14 Billy stabbed his first victim. He claimed to have found it quite easy to do. And given what came later, that is entirely credible. He was undoubtedly tough physically and backed that up whenever he thought it necessary, with the use of the 'chiv' (cut-throat razor or knife) that he always carried. Sometimes, though popular myth says otherwise, he undoubtedly resorted to firearms.

For the young Hill, violence was something to be meted out as required. As an example, when two other thugs set upon an old-time and well-respected thief called Dodger Mullins, Hill sliced both their faces, inflicting massive injuries. By now he had developed his own branding. When I say 'branding' I don't mean the way Virgin Trains or Coca Cola would use it. I mean it rather as used in the Wild West by cattle wranglers. Hill would cut a 'V' sign on his victim's face (in addition to slashing their scalp, arms or whatever took his fancy).

I have used the Dodger Mullins incident simply to show a further line of continuity. Amongst the 1981 arrests of Gentry & Others (see Chapter 3, page 40) there was one Jack (Dodger) Mullins. I remember he was a cussed old devil. He must have been in his late sixties and he treated my colleagues and me with all the respect you would save for a yapping Chihuahua. I also have little doubt that Dodger Mullins shared a good deal of DNA with the Dodger Mullins friend of Billy Hill (son perhaps?).

Years later, at my meeting with Tom Wisbey at the Grosvenor hotel in Stockbridge, Hampshire, he surprised me by bringing Dodger's name into the conversation. Tom told me that Dodger had told him, after the 1981 arrests, that he had bitterly regretted getting involved with Bill Gentry. Dodger said he should have continued to work alone 'doing the mails', which he had apparently done very successfully for many years!

This old Dodger Mullins (1980s version) has been written about elsewhere with reference to his contempt for the Kray twins. In particular, as a south London bookie, how he, Mullins, had given the Krays the boot when they tried to muscle in on his business. I have no doubt that this is a true story.

Before the Second World War, Billy Hill was at first a house-breaker and opportunist thief. The Brighton Line, like the South Coast Raiders later, was his favourite for stealing mails.

During the Second World War he made a good deal of money by avoiding conscription and getting into the business of selling black-market foodstuffs, nylons and other goods. Housebreaking, looting war-damaged properties, burglary; these were his sources of high income. By 1950, when he was 39, Hill had a fierce reputation right across London. He ran many successful criminal enterprises, most notably protection rackets, 'smash and grab', the odd kidnap and ransom, armed robbery and, of course, mailbags.

During the 1950s and '60s, Britain was a 'cash society' and that suited Hill perfectly. Vast amounts of cash were moved daily by companies such as Security Express, Securicor and, most of all, the Post Office. Armed raids were commonplace, and during this period, Billy Hill was the foremost gangster in London. But in 1952, he pulled off a remarkably spectacular and audacious robbery on a Post Office van. It was known as the 'Eastcastle Street robbery'.

Though Hill was never convicted or even charged with the crime, it is generally accepted that he was behind it. We know for instance that the Flying Squad received credible information within days that Hill was the organiser.* And, of course, we know that many years later he conceded that he was its mastermind. Why did it take him so long? Well, the money had not been recovered and there was no statute of limitations to prevent a trial even thirty years after the event.

During the 1950s, Hill made a 'killing', or rather several, and in both senses of the phrase. He was by now living a life of real luxury with regular visits to Morocco, where he had a home and a little later his own casino. With a posh flat in a fashionable part of London, and other homes in London too, he was an international traveller using both his own yacht and private flights for all sorts of criminal purposes including smuggling and later drug dealing.

---

* Cook, *The Untold Story*, p.15.

Exploring the nature of the Eastcastle Street robbery, and its leadership, sheds light on the Great Train Robbery. You might well conclude there are critical similarities.

Before arriving in Eastcastle Street, the mail van had left Paddington train station and was travelling across London. It netted him over £260,000, a massive amount for a single robbery and, at the time, the biggest street robbery in British criminal history. The currency notes were being returned to the Bank of England for cleaning or destruction according to their condition. None of the money was recovered. The money had just been offloaded from a Travelling Post Office (TPO) train at Paddington. The success of the raid depended upon inside information, careful planning, accurate timing, the use of experienced, tight-lipped robbers, speed, daring, the use of sufficient violence and audacity.

No one was ever caught, no one ever talked, the money was never recovered. One of the robbers on his team was known to be 'Tel' Hogan, but there was apparently insufficient evidence to charge him. Similarly, within days of the GTR, the names of Hill and Hogan were first on the police radar. Once again there was insufficient evidence against either, but Hogan was most definitely a known associate of Hill and members of the GTR gang, particularly Reynolds.

It is generally accepted that in his *Autobiography of a Thief* Reynolds uses 'Harry' or 'Harry Booth' as a pseudonym for Terry Hogan. In that book he describes a long-standing and trusted working relationship between the two going back to the days when Reynolds was no more than 20 years old. On Hill, Reynolds, when talking about an earlier gang that he was part of (that also included Hogan), says: 'I was the junior on the firm. … *Harry* had been part of Billy Hill's firm involved in major robberies…'.[**]

Hogan's name appears frequently in the official records and, later, books in connection with his strong associations with both Hill and Reynolds. As an example, after the GTR, when the Flying Squad

---

[**] Reynolds, *The Autobiography of a Thief*, p.191.

were searching for Reynolds, his description and the details of the car he was believed to be driving appeared in national newspapers.

A member of the public came forward with an address at which they had seen both the car and a man fitting Reynolds's description. That address, 10 Walpole Lodge, was occupied by Hogan (Cook, quoting from DPP file 2/3717 Report 16).

Hill's name crops up elsewhere in Reynolds' book too. For instance: 'London didn't have a legal casino. Instead there were house parties, most of them arranged by Billy Hill'.*

Reynolds goes on to describe how members of his gang would, under the auspices of Hill, cheat at cards: 'I ... proved useful because I wasn't a well-known face in gambling circles.' Hill's venture into gambling scams was by then well established. Reynolds also refers to another 'idol', one 'Billy G' (Billy Gentry).

As far back as his borstal days, Reynolds was dreaming of Billy Hill. Reynolds, then self-conscious about wearing spectacles, says: 'But guys like Glen Miller ... and in the nick, Billy Hill, the self-styled king of the underworld, wore a rimless pair. If it was alright for Bill, it was alright for me.'** This was hero worship.

The book is littered with references to 'Harry'. The first refers to their meeting in 1954 when Reynolds joined 'Harry' in a gang of burglars: '*Harry*, who was by far the most experienced among us, had been involved in the Eastcastle Mailbag job.'***

The Eastcastle Street robbery was extensively reported in the press, who were clearly impressed by the planning and audacity of the crime... 'Carried out "with Montgomery-like thoroughness" ... like a commando raid during the war.' Those words were not used about another crime until the GTR.

In Billy Hill's own words, this is how the Eastcastle Street job unfolded:

> At about midnight ... nine men gathered ... in a flat ... they had been told a week previously to hold themselves in

---

* Reynolds, *The Autobiography of a Thief*, p.80.

** Reynolds, *The Autobiography of a Thief*, p.53.

***Reynolds, *The Autobiography of a Thief*, p.60.

readiness … (they had each been picked up separately by car in the two hours before)… They were locked up for the time being … (then they were briefed on the job for the first time)

He told them if the job worked out there would be plenty in it for all of them. Each man had his particular role explained.

… At 2 o'clock on Tuesday morning a man (one of the gang) dressed in Post Office uniform … (armed with the registration number of a particular mail van, entered the Post Office Yard and deactivated its emergency alarm, he then left the yard) … He then crossed the road … went to a nearby telephone box and phoned the West End flat at which nine men were waiting.

At 3.30 another man was waiting at Paddington station. His job was to keep the Post Office van, now with no alarm system working, under observation. As soon as it left the station he phoned the flat.

Earlier that morning an accomplice had visited a disused garage, removed the padlock from the gates and replaced it with another padlock for which he held the keys. He drove a lorry filled with empty apple boxes into the old garage and secured the premises.

That night, cars were stolen to transport the robbers. The attack took place in Eastcastle Street; masked robbers used coshes on the postal staff who were left semi-conscious and bleeding. The robbers got clean away and drove straight to the disused garage where the mailbags full of money were transferred to the waiting lorry and driven off once again.

The money was taken to the country where it was divided between fifteen men in all.****

After the event, when questioned by the police, Hill said that he had thirty witnesses all perfectly willing to swear that he was miles away at the time of the robbery.

****   Billy Hill, *Boss of Britain's Underworld.*

The Eastcastle Street robbery was regarded as a national scandal and numerous questions were asked in the Commons and in the press about how such a raid could possibly be carried out. It is said that Prime Minister Winston Churchill became involved in the awkward questions being directed at both the Post Office and the police. It is also said, believably, that the police were under tremendous pressure to make arrests. So convinced was the *Daily Express* that Hill was behind it that it seriously contemplated publicly naming Hill, even though he had not been charged. You can understand why they might do that; Hill was so well connected to the Establishment and so brazen in his lifestyle that although 'anyone who knew anything' was certain that he was behind it, he seemed immune to arrest.

Hill got to hear about the *Express*'s plans and threatened to sue if it went ahead. Certainly the *Daily Express* was well informed, probably as a result of close contacts at the Yard. Here is one extract from that newspaper published within two days of the robbery:

> It is almost certain that one man planned the raid … A small team … are told (by him) to hand pick the raiders … they are given … an assurance that if they are caught their wives and families will be looked after. Contacts have to be made in Glasgow, London and at the scene of the crime.

You will see later that the paragraph above taken from the *Daily Express* in August 1952 might just as well have been written in August 1963.

The Eastcastle Street robbery depended on an insider, someone working in the Post Office who could provide the necessary details – how much would be carried on the train, the arrival time of the train at Paddington, the route to be taken that day by the van as it travelled across London (routes were varied), how many postmen would be protecting it, security devices fitted to the vehicle and any emergency communications that were in place. All of these things Hill had to get answers to. The identity of the insider has remained a mystery, and so has any positive evidence linking Hill to the crime.

Years after the Great Train Robbery, Hill said that he had *made sure* he was abroad at the time of the GTR; in fact he later showed that he was in the South of France with Terry Hogan.[*]

Of course you might wonder how on earth Hill and Hogan planned to make sure they had evidence of being abroad at the time of the GTR unless they were involved or at least aware well in advance of the date it would be committed. Remarkably, this simple question seems to have been ignored or overlooked since 1963!

One more point on that: appearing to have been abroad at the time of the robbery is not the same as actually being abroad. It would have been perfectly easy for Hill and Hogan to have provably travelled on a scheduled flight a few days before the GTR. Then they could have sneaked back using stolen or false passports, or using a private flight, in order to participate before making a swift and silent return to France. How do we know this could have been on their agenda? Well, it is precisely what Gordon Goody intended with his (alibi) trip to Ireland (see later). I am not suggesting that Hill was present at the scene of the robbery; he would have had no need to be. However, Hogan is a different matter.

Later, Hill claimed that the coshing of the mail van driver in Eastcastle Street was not severe and that no real damage was done, rather like the claims by those who coshed Driver Mills about ten years later. My contention is that the Eastcastle Street job gave Hill an even bigger idea. Why not steal the money from the TPO train away from the closed environment of Central London? After all, if he could stop the train on its journey in a quiet secluded spot, one in which the police would remain oblivious to the crime for perhaps an hour or more, he could steal the lot. This was the theory I shared with Tom Wisbey and which, thanks to the use of the device of 'fiction' (see later), he reluctantly agreed with.

During the late 1950s, the Flying Squad began to have greater success in detecting attacks on security vehicles on the

---

[*] Russell-Pavier/Richards, *Crime of the Century*, p.60.

streets. Thus attacks on road mail vans were somewhat replaced by attacks on mail trains, in which the Flying Squad had little interest. As already discussed in Chapter 4, for many detectives, diverting criminals onto the railways was a positive thing.

By late 1962, attacks on mail trains had grown significantly and an expertise in stopping and robbing trains had been developed by the South Coast Raiders.

Many people hold that Tom Wisbey was related through marriage to Billy Hill, but whether that was true or not I do not know. Tom was not keen to dwell on the subject although his daughter Marilyn says that they were related.

I believe that, by late 1962, Billy shared his idea to rob a TPO with trusted enforcers whom he would use as a line of communication to the robbers. Why would it be necessary to put a 'wall' between himself and the large gang of robbers? Well, Hill was known to be at the top of the criminal 'pile' and there were a thousand informers who gladly kept the police abreast of Hill's contacts and meetings. And in any event, Hill is known to have been paranoid about the security of his operations, and with good cause.

In his book *Boss of Britain's Underworld*, Hill says he thought, perhaps rightly, that his office was bugged, his telephone tapped, that police informers were deployed to gather information on him and that he and his associates were under constant police surveillance. He was probably right on all counts. It would have been virtually impossible for him to regularly meet with, or otherwise talk to, a group of known armed robbers and mailbag thieves. So, other than by use of trusted lieutenants, he could not possibly:

a)   give instructions to such individuals as to how the plan was to be carried out;

b)   ensure that everyone knew well in advance that in the event of any member of the GTR gang being arrested, there would be devastating reprisals if they implicated Hill or other members of the gang;

c)   remain undetected.

The only way Hill could safely organise and manage the GTR was to stay completely hidden behind his enforcers and to be very publicly abroad during its execution. This he did.

Fordham does not name Hill, but she did conduct confidential interviews with at least two of the robbers (Ronnie Biggs and one other) and was adept at putting diverse comments together. She was confident enough to propose that the mastermind was someone with whom Reynolds was friendly, and spent time with, in the South of France.[*] That fits perfectly, given: that Reynolds had known Hill for several years; that Hill visited the South of France with Reynolds' friend Terry Hogan; and that Reynolds spoke of visiting that very area.

Fordham also states her belief that if the mastermind took his cut of the loot abroad then it probably went to a man waiting in Morocco or Gibraltar.[**] Of course, Morocco was Hill's second home and Gibraltar was well known to him. As she points out, those two locations were frequently mentioned in the 'voluminous' evidence at the trail.

So, if I am right and Hill was behind it all, who did he use as his trusted lieutenants or enforcers? It might have been the Harris brothers. I know you have never heard of them. But Tom Wisbey told me quite enthusiastically that they were a pretty 'heavy duty' bunch who had associated with the South Coast Raiders and would definitely have been keen to participate. That's the problem. Tom offered me their names without any hesitation or concern. In other words, it wasn't them! But he simply never spoke that way when he was making a true revelation about the involvement of Danny Pembroke, or what I believe to be true about Freddie Sansom, Billy Hill, or the involvement of a bent copper.

But with the Krays it was different. Most people hated them, and they seem to have hated back pretty strongly too. Certainly they were East Enders and had distanced themselves from South London villains, regarding that area of London as 'Indian

---

[*] Fordham, *The Robbers' Tale*, p.41.
[**] Fordham, *The Robbers' Tale*, p.41.

country'. Did Tom Wisbey ever admit the Krays were involved? Well, he certainly wasn't keen to. It was more that he acquiesced 'for the sake of the story'. The question is, what evidence exists to suggest that they were?

Before turning to the evidence, it is possible there may be some readers asking, 'Who were the Krays?' Well, there were three Kray brothers: the twins, Reggie and Ronnie, and their older brother, Charlie. Here I am concerned with the twins.

They were born in 1933, raised in the East End of London and took to amateur boxing at a young age. By the time of their fall in the mid/late 1960s they were well known as the first real celebrity gangsters. They had bullied, murdered, deceived and cheated their way across the East End and West End of London. Their empire started with ownership of a scruffy billiard hall in Bethnal Green and gradually expanded to clubs and bars across East London and the West End. The billiard hall was for a long time their centre of operations. There, Ronnie, a dangerous and unpredictable maniac, cherished an arsenal of guns, knives and other weapons. The billiard hall quickly became a den of thieves and was frequented by the likes of Buster Edwards, Gordon Goody and certain others who became Great Train Robbers.

The Krays provided a service to their dishonest customers: they acted as minders for stolen property (at a price), and illicit profits (at a price); helped set one thief up with another (for a cut); and provided a safe place where villains could talk out of earshot of the public and the police. But to their enemies – and there were plenty across London, and south London in particular – they were thieves' 'ponces', dangerous, unpredictable, dishonest and distasteful. To the top villains of south London, the twins were dismissed as 'Gert and Daisy'. That, along with their overwhelming ambition, ultimately led to a murderous conflict and their downfall. The Krays also ran protection rackets, 'long firm frauds', stole from thieves and followed any pursuit where quick money could be made.

Both twins were prone to extreme and unforeseen violence. The infliction of grievous bodily harm, torture and the

Ronnie Kray with his friend and confidant, Lord Boothby.

commission of murder was part of their trade. It was carried out whenever thought necessary by the twins and their 'Firm' (as it was known). Certainly, both twins suffered with mental illness, but Ronnie was so seriously ill that he was eventually consigned to Broadmoor hospital. Both died after serving part of long custodial sentences.

Nevertheless, during the late 1950s and increasingly during the early 1960s, their company was shared by David Bailey, the celebrity photographer, George Raft, Hollywood movie star and alleged mafia contact, Barbara Windsor, Frank Sinatra, Judy Garland and many more. They also had fans at the House of Lords, Lord Boothby for instance, and in other places of significant influence including the House of Commons, e.g. Tom Driberg MP. All that is well established.

Ronnie Kray, the more unhinged of the twins, liked to be referred to as 'The Colonel', and what Ronnie wanted, Ronnie usually got, at least from those who sought his favours, or wished to avoid his anger. It might be that this reveals some personality trait that Ronnie shared with Bruce Reynolds. During the GTR Reynolds dressed as an army officer. Is there more to be read into their respective adopted ranks? Was Reynolds signifying that in terms of organisational structure, he saw himself as in the immediate reporting line to Ronnie?

As you would expect after over fifty years, any direct proof of the Krays' hidden involvement in the GTR is extremely unlikely to surface. I could tell you that Tom Wisbey told me in detail about the meetings he had with Reggie and Ronnie at which the planning of the robbery took place. I could tell you that he told me that the Krays moved their HQ to their new Glenrae Hotel in 1963 (on the Seven Sisters Road in the East End), specifically to cater for meetings with the GTR robbery team. It was a unique venue with enough bedrooms and other facilities to enable the GTR gang to sleep, meet and plan in secret. The basement bar could accommodate a score of men and was more private and less able to be bugged, or viewed, than any other place in their growing empire.

All I can offer you is the tacit agreement of a reluctant, now deceased witness (Tom Wisbey) that Hill and the Krays were involved. My assertions are based on that plus logic and some circumstantial evidence. I have already mentioned that I have had custody of the entire Metropolitan Police file on the case. I did not read it all as time and need did not allow, but I did not read anything in that file to suggest the involvement of the Krays. That does not concern me. There are good reasons why, even if the Krays were involved, no formal record might have been made. It is possible that reference to the Krays was there somewhere in that huge file waiting to be found. I don't know.

Remember too as you consider their potential involvement, that the notorious Freddie Foreman worked for many years for Billy Hill and he was the Krays' right-hand man. He was also godfather to Tom Wisbey's daughter (Marilyn). In fact, Freddie Foreman seems to have been close not only with the twins but also their older brother Charlie and their mother Vie too. His speciality was cleaning up the bodies after Reggie and Ronnie had done any butchering. But Freddie was also an armed robber, ex railway man and long-time friend of Billy Hill. His sisters were close with Buster Edwards and Tom Wisbey. In addition, Mad Frankie Frazer was in a long-term relationship with Marilyn Wisbey and he was one of Billy Hill's most trusted enforcers.

Marilyn Wisbey says that her mother, Renee Wisbey (née Hill), was related to Billy Hill. Some good sources have stated this as a proven fact. For instance: 'Tommy Wisbey's father-in-law was the cousin of another notorious London gangster, Billy Hill'.[*]

Of course, most of the robbers and the Krays were all known to one another. It is clear that virtually all of the Great Train Robbers, and that means Goody's gang (sometimes called the South West gang) and members of the South Coast Raiders gang, were familiar to each other for years before the big event. Billy Hill and the Krays were in the middle of that social and criminal mix too.

The robbers knew one another through childhood school friendships, and/or reputations, and/or attending the same social venues (nightclubs, snooker halls, dance halls, dog tracks, West End restaurants, and/or being in prison or borstal together, or through mutual friends). Members of both gangs had on occasions worked together as partners in crime. By 1960, they were all part of a particular group of determined, violent and seasoned 'faces' who frequented, and socialised in:

> a string of clubs in the West End, including the Cabinet Club … Stork club … and Log Cabin … (where) the potent cocktail of cabaret, late-night booze and hostesses attracted … the likes of the Krays, Freddie Foreman, Frankie Frazer and Billy Hill.[**]

For instance, the relationship between Tom Wisbey's family and Frankie Frazer is well known, and so, of course, is the fact that Frankie was very close to, and regularly employed by Billy Hill. In

---

[*] Russell-Pavier/Richards, *Crime of the Century*, location 630.
[**] Russell-Pavier/Richards, *Crime of the Century*.

addition, Frankie Frazer said, and I can tell you that Tom Wisbey did not deny it, that he was invited to take part in the GTR. Frazer did not disclose who it was that invited him – it might have been Wisbey, but it could equally have been, if my contention is correct, Billy Hill, 'Tel' Hogan or the Krays. We do know, because official records and Reynolds himself tell us, that by the time of the GTR, Bruce Reynolds had been working regularly with Terry Hogan, one of Hill's close lieutenants.

The relationship between Hill and the Krays has often been described. See, for instance, *Bringing Down the Krays* by Bobby Teale: 'The Vienna Rooms in the Edgeware Road is where the old faces like Jack Spot and Billy Hill used to hang out – and where the Krays used to come and learn from the masters.' And later: 'The word was they'd (the Krays) flown off to Tangier in Morocco to live it up in the sun with the old villain, Billy Hill.'

It is clear that the Krays in their late teens and early twenties saw Billy Hill as their idol. And by 1966 the relationship had developed so much that when the twins were in serious trouble:

> They had an escape route… and a private aircraft was waiting for them in a field near Bognor … they flew on without incident to Morocco … three untroubled weeks … Billy (Hill) was there, a respected figure in his big white car to show them around … Reggie spoke of buying a small club (there).[*]

There is good evidence to be found of collaboration between the Krays and Billy Hill for anyone who cares to do a little research. For instance, the book *Tangier: City of the Dream* by Ian Finlayson (Harper Collins, 1992) says much about Tangier that is not about crime or criminals but mentions in passing, when talking about Tangier in the late 1950s: 'Billy Hill, a substantial London gangster, virtual Godfather to the menacing Kray twins, had taken up residence in the city … Hill maintained an interest in several

---

[*] John Pearson, *Profession of Violence*, p.225.

matters ... he had recruited the Kray brothers, Ronnie and Reginald, to supervise his remaining business interests'.**

That author goes on to describe how Ronnie Kray was made to feel at home by Billy in his Tangier flat where a little piece of London had been recreated. He says Ronnie was 27 years old at the time.*** The twins were born in 1933, making this close relationship between them and Hill a full three years before the Great Train Robbery.

Importantly, Ronnie Kray flew to Glasgow several times in 1963 to meet with Glasgow gangsters.**** And so did Bruce Reynolds and (his brother-in-law) John Daly.***** I should remind you at this point that I have had access to records that no other writer on this subject has had. Since 1963, many official papers have been held back from view. Periodically, some are released; gradually the truth is exposed. That process continues, though a mountain of papers on the Krays and Billy Hill are still hidden from public view. If the public had had access fifteen years ago to the totality of GTR papers then much of the nonsense that has been created and promulgated would not exist to confuse the picture.

Let me put that rant to one side. Regarding the Krays, it cannot be doubted that in 1963 they would have been delighted to be part of any major crime that their hero and associate, Hill, was planning. And it can be easily shown that the robbers also knew the Krays long before the GTR (apart from Cordrey and Ronnie Biggs). For instance, in *How to Rob a Train* Gordon Goody explains that by the time of the robbery he had known the Krays for years. He describes how he, in about 1955, 'bumped into a young East End hard nut Ronnie Kray in the snooker hall. It was the first time I'd met him.'****** And the association between train robbers and the Kray family did not stop in 1963. I can say with absolute certainty, as described in Chapter 3, that members

**	Finlayson *Tangier*, p.304.
***	Finlayson *Tangier*, p.306.
****	John Pearson, *Profession of Violence*, p.184–85.
*****	Cook quoting Post Office file 'POST 120/95')
******	Goody, *How to Rob a Train*, p.34.

of the old Kray firm were still involved with former train robbers right up until the 1980s.

My final point is this: in 1963, no other firm of enforcers in London better fitted the job description that Hill was trying to fill. Some may ask, what about the Richardsons? The answer to that is simple: the south London Richardsons were too close to members of the South Coast Raiders; not so the East End boys. As Pearson points out:

> The(ir) rackets varied but the twins' role remained the same – they were the source of fear, the men behind the scenes whose names guaranteed results. If things went wrong lesser men took the rap. No one would denounce them, betrayal was unthinkable.[*]

Many people think of the Krays as living their business lives within the East End and West End of London. But in reality, they had definite connections with, and visited, the gangsters of Glasgow (where of course the TPO started its journey).

Arthur Thompson, the leading figure in organised crime in Glasgow for over twenty years, was a young man in 1963, but by then he had already built a reputation as a man of extreme violence and was getting rich quick through running protection rackets. The connection between the Krays and Thompson has in recent years been exposed. See, for instance, *Blink, A Journey Through Gangland Mayhem* by David Leslie (Mainstream Publishing), Chapter 20, plus *The Krays, The Final Countdown* by Colin Fry (Mainstream Publishing).

As I have shown, the Krays' relationship with Glasgow goes back to 1963 and perhaps earlier. 'The spring of 1963 was a good period for the Krays … with their success at organising criminals.' That year, 'They were riding high and expanding – betting shops, restaurants, tobacconists, and a security firm specialising in the transport and security of valuables.'[**]

---

[*]   Pearson, *Profession of Violence*, p. 180.
[**] Pearson, *Profession of Violence*.

Within two years of the GTR, there was open warfare between the Kray Firm and the Richardson brothers from south of the river. In describing this, Pearson says that in the fight against the Richardsons, the Krays had the help of two brothers who led a gang of thieves from Clapham who had been closely involved in the GTR.***

However, you still might choose to disregard the evidence and logical conclusions that can be drawn from the above that Hill and the Krays were behind the Great Train Robbery. I think any reasonable person would be hard pressed not to conclude that someone was pulling the strings. It seems to me there is only one other contender: Gordon Goody.

There is no doubt that Goody had a forcible personality and the strength to exert his will by violent means if required. But, did he have the intelligence, the 'pull' or the necessary knowledge? In his autobiography, while describing how to plan a robbery, Goody states: 'The two essential ingredients for success are reliable information and trustworthy associates.'**** I guess you don't have to be a very experienced leader or manager to ask, 'What about planning?' Is it possible that a man who has masterminded the GTR, with all the planning that such an undertaking required, could possibly think that 'planning' is not a key ingredient, or perhaps be stupid enough to forget that he had done a great deal of it?

Goody was not the mastermind; he was the foreman. In an indirect way he seems to have confirmed that to Fordham. She writes that Goody 'boasted that they were pulled in for every big job'.***** The unasked and obvious question is apparent: pulled in by whom? All in all, I think there is good reason to suppose that Goody was not 'Mr Big'.

Shortly after the robbery, certainly before most of the robbers had been arrested, a suspicious death occurred on the Underground. Bert Bundy, a solicitor's clerk who was well known amongst the less salubrious members of the press, was

---

***   Pearson, *Profession of Violence*, p. 216.
****   Goody, *How to Rob a Train*, p. 78.
*****   Goody, *How to Rob a Train*, p. 73.

attempting to sell a story that he 'knew both the brain behind the mail train robbery and those concerned in it'.[*] Note again the separation: 'knew both the brain behind the mail train robbery *and* those concerned in it'.

Mr Bundy died of head injuries; there were no witnesses and the coroner returned an open verdict. I've attended more than enough coroners' courts to know that coroners hate open verdicts. It says, 'I wasn't able to establish how this person died.' Was it murder? Or was it perhaps just a coincidence? Was it suicide? There is absolutely no reason to think so. Was it an accident? Perhaps he was half drunk. Did he trip and fall? The coroner saw no evidence to support that verdict. Even if the poor devil was murdered, it doesn't prove that the Krays and Billy Hill were responsible. However, if you believe that they were involved in the GTR, then you have to conclude, if it was murder, then Hill ordered it and the Krays orchestrated it.

What can be concluded with certainty is that the GTR was at least many months, if not well over a year, in the planning. It was a massive enterprise in terms of its ambition and scale. Can you imagine any police informant (of which there were thousands in the capital) not wanting to inform? What informant would not want to be the one with the information on the crime of the century? Think of the potential for reward.

Yet no informer came forward with a credible reason for naming Hill. This is because Hill was known for his paranoia and the care he therefore took with information security. Secondly, those that knew or suspected anything about Hill's involvement would be very aware that they would be extremely sorry if any leak was attributed to them.

Fordham clearly believes that any ordinary person, on reading the evidence of the robbery without preconceptions, would conclude that there was a mastermind who was not present at the robbery but who planned the attack in detail. From all she had heard and could reasonably deduce, she concluded that the

---

[*]   Fordham, *The Robbers' Tale*, p.34.

mastermind was at the top of his violent profession: brutal, paranoid and content with an even share of the loot.[**]

I believe all the evidence now, as then, points to that same conclusion.

I have a piece of notepaper in my possession that might be significant in all this. Tom Wisbey handwrote it. It was left in a book that I had with me when we met in Stockbridge. It stayed there, forgotten until this year (2019) when I picked the book up again for the first time since it came into my possession. It is reproduced on the following page, but it simply says:

> Jim gave a fellow a right hand, he was with me and Danny at
> the time went over to see Bill at the time at Churchills Club
> where Bill was minding the door at the time.
> We used to go over to see Bill.
> Harry H. Corbett – Meeting a girl.
> Phone call from Bill asking for me and Danny to meet him re
> the Krays
>
> Graham,
> A short note here the book as promised. I've wrote a few notes
> for you? So I won't forget, and I will discuss it when I see you
> regarding it.
>   Tom.

As you can see there is reference to a 'Billy', a 'Danny', 'Churchills Club' and the 'Krays'. I have no doubt that 'Danny' is Danny Pembroke, and I have no doubt that 'Krays' refers to the twins. The only Billy we ever discussed at length was Billy Hill. Churchill's was the name of Billy Hill's club/casino in Tangier but also the name of a London club, so I cannot be certain that it refers to Hill's casino. 'Minding the door' refers to providing 'protection' (of the sort within the meaning of 'protection racket').

[**] Fordham, *The Robbers' Tale*, p.25–27.

Handwritten note to me from Tom Wisbey.

It's disappointing that I didn't take the opportunity to discuss the note with Tom. A hundred questions arise. For instance, I would certainly have liked to know if he had been to Morocco like some of the other train robbers, and I would also like to have known more about his meetings with Hill and any involvement with the Krays.

As you would expect, I asked Marilyn Wisbey if she had ever asked her father about 'Mr Big'. She told me that her father was always reluctant to tell her anything about his 'professional' life. In years gone by he had simply ignored her questions. But more recently he had, for the first time ever, confided in her that there really was one man behind the 'job'. You can imagine, that having discovered that, Marilyn followed it up with more questions, firstly, 'Who was it?' Tom obviously resorted to his habitual response. He told her he had never met him and didn't know.

Writing just after the main GTR trial, Fordham says, 'the police throughout have persistently denied the existence of a master brain.' She goes on, 'This is beginning to be the stock version of the story.' How right she was.[*]

The existence of a mastermind was clear to her, yet there was a vacuum where the identity and background of the obvious suspect should have been given.

---

[*] Fordham, *The Robbers' Tale*, p.25.

TEN

NOT ONE PLAN BUT TWO

At first it seems the robbery was viewed as a masterpiece of planning and execution. As the years went by, that view appears to have dimmed. More recently, there has been the view that all they did was stick a glove over a red signal. However, if you look closely at the detail of the robbery and the potential for error, you begin to appreciate a great deal of work must have gone into the planning. Potential critical errors include:

a) high-security TPO coach being in use;

b) an attack when the payload was light;

c) a leak during the many months of the planning from within a team of more than sixteen;

d) a train passing by during the robbery and its driver informing the next encountered signal box staff;

e) the early arrival of any 'linesman' called out to inspect/repair the signal/phone and thereby stumbling into the crime in action (see Chapter 13);

f) the wrong timing of the next fast train on that route – with the possibility of a false red signal causing a collision;

g) raising suspicions in the mind of the signalman once he became aware that signals had failed, and a very valuable and vulnerable train had made an unscheduled stop in his 'section';

h) failing to plan adequately for the response of the train guard on the train attacked.

But contrast the plan for the actual attack with the utter mayhem that occurred once all the mailbags were loaded to the getaway vehicles:

a) One of the robbers warned the postal staff not to move for thirty minutes. From this the police rightly judged that the hideaway was within thirty minutes' drive. A key mistake by the robbers.

b) The chaos of each individual robber making a dash from Leatherslade Farm having stayed there long enough to arouse suspicions and be seen.

c) Leaving behind at Leatherslade Farm enough forensic evidence to keep a dozen scientists, fingerprint experts and scenes of crimes officers busy for three months.

d) Individual robbers, each of whom had a face well known to those searching for them, making off from the farm carrying tens of thousands of pounds of stolen money.

Would anyone of average intelligence, after a year of planning, want to hurriedly hide, or abandon a fortune, the discovery of which would lead to a lifetime of imprisonment?

It seems clear that there was a thorough plan for the robbery itself but a definite absence of planning to protect the robbers 'on the ground' after the money was obtained.

Fordham says:

> From the very beginning it was laid down that each man was to be responsible for himself and was to make arrangements for his own share … Disposal (of the money) was bound to be the crux of a successful enterprise.[*]

And yet:

> A brain as good as that which had planned the scheme itself would have worked out a method which should have been

---

[*] Fordham, *The Robbers' Tale*, p.40.

able to get the men and money away, in all probability, before the alarm was given.**

More cynically, perhaps the mastermind was convinced that the authorities would be satisfied if the 'foot soldiers' were captured. Goodness, you even had one who wanted to dress up as an SAS major and pretend he was in charge. What better eager fool could you find?

Whatever the motivation, it really does seem there were two plans. The first was for the robbery itself, and the second for the mastermind to get his share away quickly.

A kinder interpretation would be to see the chaos as inevitable. After all, it is stretching credulity to think that the robbers at the scene would have been happy for all the money (uncounted) to be moved immediately in bulk to a remote location whilst they toddled off elsewhere. No, you can imagine that each would want to know immediately how much they had 'made', and each would want immediate possession of their share.

So, if you were the mastermind, what would you have done with your eighteenth share? Perhaps it would be driven straight back to London, or perhaps it would have been hidden elsewhere. Apparently, the gang had prepared a heavy ex-army lorry, with a hidden compartment for three shares of the money. It seems this was to go straight from the scene of the robbery, but to where? This has never been disclosed; the lorry was evidently disregarded byt the robbers at the farm when it became unusable.

Perhaps the mastermind had a light aircraft to whisk it away from a disused airfield close to the scene, straight to his place in Morocco. Was there such an airfield? Yes. Did Billy Hill have a place in Morocco? Yes. Did the Krays visit Morocco? Yes. Did some of the train robbers visit Morocco? Yes. But would Billy Hill have had the wherewithal to organise a secret private flight? Don't be daft! And at the trial itself did Brian and

---

** Fordham, *The Robbers' Tale*, p.50.

Karen Field★ both swear in evidence that they visited Tangier in August 1963? Yes.

Today, a trip to Morocco would not be viewed by many people as particularly exotic, adventurous or strange. Now many Brits have travelled to Southern Europe and beyond. North Africa, the Middle East, Asia, America: none of these places is anything but fairly routine. But in the early 1960s, things were really very different. Most men went to work on a bike (leaving their wives at home). An annual holiday for the vast majority of families in those days involved a week in the nearest seaside resort. It would be Skegness, Brighton, Southend, Blackpool, Rhyl or some such place. For the ordinary working family, Europe, and certainly Morocco, would have been out of the question. Remember too that this was the year that the Krays set up their freight business, and, of course, Billy Hill also had his famous seagoing yacht.

Lack of any real planning in terms of how the robbers' shares would be safely managed was an obviously fatal blunder. As Fordham says, 'disposal was bound to be the crux of a successful enterprise … (yet it) was never properly organised from the top as it ought to have been.'

It was the share-out that caused all the trouble and led to the early arrest of Cordrey, for instance. For, if the robbers had ripped out the back seats of high-powered saloon cars and loaded them with loot they could have been in South London before the alarm was raised. If they had prepared a large enough hole in the ground half an hour's drive north, then the loot could have been buried and left for six months. If there had been adequate post-robbery planning, then individual robbers would not have been carting huge amounts of money around the country looking for somewhere to hide it. Roger Cordrey was arrested in Bournemouth within forty-eight hours. He had unwittingly approached a retired police officer's wife and asked if he could

---

★ Brian Field was a dishonest young solicitor's clerk who helped organise the purchase of the robbers' hideaway at Leatherslade Farm. He was well known to Gordon Goody prior to the robbery and had previously helped in his defence in relation to other matters. He served approximately four years in jail for his part in the affair. Karen was Brian's wife.

rent her garage, and then attempted to pay from a wedge of used notes. All of those obvious errors are in stark contrast to the careful planning that led to the successful attack. Other money was found hidden in a caravan, some was hidden in door panels, some was dumped in a phone box in central London, another stash was found abandoned in woods.

The discipline that kept the plan to rob the train secret, and that had resulted in a successful robbery, was clearly abandoned as soon as the robbers got back to Leatherslade Farm.

That did not trouble the mastermind. His money had already moved to hands that were never anywhere near the scene of the robbery. As Fordham states: 'The hideout was for the lesser robbers.'** And, 'Why was there the extraordinary discrepancy between the skill of the robbery itself and the debacle of Leatherslade Farm? Why did the intelligence which had directed the one, give out over the other?'***

** Fordham, *The Robbers' Tale*, p.50.
*** Fordham, *The Robbers' Tale*, p.15.

ELEVEN

ONE GANG, TWO ELEMENTS

Certainly, no one knows exactly how well all of those involved in the robbery knew one another. Indeed, no one knows for certain the full cast of players. But two things are clear. Firstly, one of the unwritten rules of professional criminals is 'Never work with a "mystery".' In other words, never work with a person who is not personally known to you. Secondly, two gangs came together to commit the GTR and most of them were definitely not strangers to one another. For example, Tom Wisbey and Buster Edwards had both been part of an earlier gang that worked for years with the infamous Freddie Foreman.

The South Coast Raiders comprised: Danny Pembroke, Roger Cordrey, Bob Welch, Tom Wisbey and, certainly in the early life of the gang, members of the Harris family and Sansoms too. I also suspect that Jim Hussey assisted them from time to time. I have called the other gang 'Goody's Gang'. It comprised: Gordon Goody, Bruce Reynolds, Buster Edwards, Charlie Wilson, Jimmy White, John Daly and Roy James. Those two separate gangs were stealing mailbags for two years and more prior to the GTR.

A week after the robbery, DCS Butler of the Flying Squad had a list of eighteen individuals he had good cause to suspect might have been responsible. They were:

Goody, Wilson, Reynolds, White, James, Welch, Daly PLUS
Kehoe, Hayden Smith, Henry (Harry) Smith, Terry Sansom,
George Sansom, Robinson, Ambrose, Cramer, Shakeshaft, Pitts.*

★ Cook, *The Untold Story.*

It is an interesting list and noteworthy now because of the presence of all the key members of the Goody/Reynolds gang and the complete absence of the key players in the South Coast Raiders. In addition, it is worth mentioning that although Freddie Sansom is not present, both of his brothers are.

Finally, it is clear that this was a first list of suspects that had yet to be properly analysed. It soon evolved. But at that time, half the list had solid alibis, none more so than the infamous Pitts, who had died in prison about a year earlier.

Yet when all the charges in connection with the GTR were finally put to those who had been arrested, and every one of them had appeared before the courts and had been sentenced, the court remained certain that others had escaped. They called those who had evaded capture Mr One, Mr Two and Mr Three. These three men were said to have been at the scene of the robbery but were never identified.

Of course, Daly was part of the robbery gang and wrongly acquitted. It seems he must be properly regarded as 'Mr One, Mr Two or Mr Three'.

I have not mentioned above Ronnie Biggs or 'Peter' (or 'Stan' or 'Pop'), the train driver allegedly supplied by Biggs via Reynolds. Biggs is omitted because he adds as much to this story as he did to the success of the GTR.

We can only know Biggs' character from his minor previous convictions, the low regard in which he was held by the other robbers and the comments of the judge at the trial ('Facile and specious liar'). Ironically, I want to separate him from the others because of a fault that he *didn't* seem to possess: he was not a hardened violent criminal.

But of the remainder, none was a 'Raffles' type thief. None would hesitate in using extreme violence, and most of them provably had on previous occasions. None seemed to ever want to knuckle down to regular, daily, hard work like the rest of us have to. It is, after all, the only way that any society can create shared wealth on which to thrive. None felt disgrace at the idea of living off the earnings of ordinary people (which of course thieves do). None felt ashamed at a lack of contribution to society, and none seemed to be aware that every crime they committed had individual, real-life victims.

Often their crimes had long-term adverse personal consequences. How many of us know or remember that the young Second Man David Whitby, aged 26, who accompanied Driver Mills that night, died of a heart attack in his early thirties? How many of us know that Frank Fuggall, who was the senior postman on the train that night, was adversely affected for the rest of his service? According to long-since-retired postal worker Geoff Higginbotham, with whom I have spoken, 'after the robbery, whenever Frank was on a TPO and it stopped unexpectedly, he would shake uncontrollably.'

And of course, every police investigation and incarceration has to be paid for by the working taxpayer.

After the GTR, all those convicted, from both gangs, were for the rest of their lives marked out as dangerous men. Most, if not all, died in poor circumstances. Frail human beings, able to show love, fear, insecurity, pride, aspiration and hope, some of them certainly were. Heroes of any type they were definitely not.

Goody's gang, of course, comprised similar men to the South Coast Raiders (except Cordrey who was different). They were all of similar backgrounds – geographically and socially – with similar education, similar taste in entertainment, similar desire to get rich quick, similar avoidance of lawful employment and similar propensity to dishonesty and violence. But the Goody gang was different in three respects: a quicker resort to violence, a lack of technical knowledge and less ability to keep the nature of their 'work' secret.

It is apparent when you look at the detail of the information Scotland Yard was receiving after the robbery that it was members of the Goody gang who were first put forward by informants. If we look at what is known of the exploits of Goody's gang, we get some measure of their expertise and the truthfulness and accuracy of their later pronouncements.

In his book *How to Rob A Train*, Goody states: 'The Irish mail train left Paddington every week, it carried the wages of Irish construction workers back to their families in Ireland.'* He goes on to describe attacking that train to get at the payroll otherwise bound for the workers in Swindon, Wiltshire. He says his gang visited Paddington and kept observations and watched the metal boxes being loaded onto the train. One of the gang discovered an abandoned factory at West Drayton (just a few miles out of Paddington, on the line to Swindon), which they could use as their getaway point. Apparently, they had a dummy run, and used the communication cord to stop the train at the designated spot (opposite the disused factory). It is said that the train came to a stop exactly at the right point.

Soon thereafter Goody, Reynolds, Wilson, Edwards and someone he calls 'Bill Jennings', undertook the real thing. It unfolded like an old Marx Brothers comedy film. While the getaway driver waited at the factory, the rest of the gang boarded the train at Paddington. Soon afterwards they jemmied open the guard's brake (no key!), assaulted the guard and tied him up. Then, Goody says, they opened the sliding doors and got ready to unload the 'seven or eight' heavy metal boxes. When the time was right they pulled the communication cord as they had done before. Then they waited... and the train rattled passed the disused factory and the getaway car for about 450 yards before stopping.

Determined to make off with the loot, despite the distance and weight of the several metal boxes, they unloaded the stolen property onto the trackside. Unfortunately for them, they had jumped off the train close to a gang of railway workers who quickly realised what was going on.

There is not much to be found on and around railway lines, but one thing that is always accessible in great quantities is ballast. Immediately Reynolds, Goody and the other master crooks came under a hail of heavy stones. Nevertheless, our dodgy folk heroes tried to hump away the goodies, but it was impossible – with or without the incessant missiles. In the end they managed to escape with just one box containing £700. Not bad shared between seven top crack thieves!

---

* Goody, *How to Rob a Train*, pp.56–57.

Now, there are two good reasons to repeat that account:

1. In the two-year run up to the GTR, Goody's gang were pretty clueless. Apart from the case reported above, there is also, amongst others, an attempt to stop a TPO in Essex using British Railways' emergency detonators. It is very clear this gang needed the South Coast Raiders much more than the Raiders needed them.

2. The Goody gang obviously did not know how to stop a train at a pre-determined place.

Much more importantly, however, is the fact that Goody repeatedly refers to the fiasco of the attack on the Swindon wages as the 'Irish Mail Train' job. However, the Irish Mail Train job, which it seems Goody did take part in, was in reality committed much later, in February 1963, as described in the chapter that follows. (Don't confuse either with the Irish Mail attack described in Chapter 4, which took place over two years earlier.)

The Irish Mail job in 1963 that Goody took part in actually took place at an entirely different location on a different region of BR at a different time of day, using a different means to stop the train and with an intention to steal high-value mail, not workers' wages. How could he make this fundamental blunder? There are three possible explanations:

a) He was so befuddled by the time he wrote his book that he was completely confused.
b) He and his gang did not plan or lead on the Irish Mail Robbery or the Great Train Robbery and were largely clueless.
c) A combination of (a) and (b) above.
d) He was intentionally trying to mislead. But to what avail?

On Friday, 26 January 1962, on an isolated stretch of railway in Essex, detonators placed on the line caused a freight train to make an emergency stop. A few minutes later a mail train passed by unharmed and the Goody gang had to watch their target train continue on its journey.[*]

Some other failed attempts are described in the books written by various members of Goody's gang and, of course, by Goody himself.

One thing we can be certain of is that the Goody gang would not hesitate to use unnecessary violence. One example is the vicious November 1962 robbery at Heathrow Airport. In that case Goody, Wilson, Reynolds, James plus others, allegedly including Terry Hogan (that trusted employee of Billy Hill again) and White got away with £62,000 before several of them were arrested. Sadly, they were not all convicted.

---

[*] Cook, *The Untold Story.*

TWELVE

THE IRISH MAIL

The Irish Mail Train Robbery of 20 February 1963 has been almost entirely overlooked. Yet it is vital in understanding the commission of the Great Train Robbery.

It took place during the worst winter in living memory, when the temperature was minus 20 in places and deep snow-drifts, up to 7 yards deep, were everywhere. On the evening of that day, Train Guard Owen left Euston Station aboard the Irish Mail bound for Holyhead. He was accompanied by the following staff: Tom John Thomas (Ticket Collector and Sleeping Car Attendant), Len Tappy (Dining Car Supervisor), Tommy Thomas and Michael Carey (Dining Car Staff), Will George Davies (Driver) and Llew Roberts (Second Man). There were, therefore, five rail staff in the coaches and two more on the locomotive.

The old LMS train had fourteen burgundy coaches with com-partmentalised carriages, each containing six passenger seats, plus a sleeping car at the front and a guard's van at the rear. All were being pulled by a BR D-type diesel locomotive.

The train set off at 8.40 p.m. carrying passengers as well as high-value mail bound for Ireland. As the train headed north out of London, the robbers were already aboard and all seemed to be going as they had planned.

There can be no doubt that the robbers carried out a surveil-lance operation on the train before deciding how best to attack it. The resultant plan was simple, but it depended on establishing the length of time the guard would spend away from the guard's brake (and the mailbags) upon leaving Euston whilst engaged in checking passengers' tickets.

During the period of his absence they would simply unlock and enter the guard's brake from the adjoining passenger coach and steal as many high-value packages as possible. They would place those stolen packages into holdalls, or suitcases, and leave the brake before the guard's return. Finally, they would await the unscheduled stop (organised by Roger Cordrey) at red lights near Tring, leave the train under cover of darkness and make their way on foot the short distance to the nearby roadway. Waiting cars would whisk them back to London. By the time the police had attended the scene of the false red signal, the robbers would be tucked up in bed at home in south London with a great deal of loot to count in the morning! Easy. What could possibly go wrong?

They had failed to take account of one vitally important factor: the awful weather. In such diabolical conditions people do not travel unless they have to, and the process of checking tickets becomes a much faster one.

Shortly after the train left Euston, Guard Owen locked the door to the guard's brake and set off up the train to meet with the ticket inspector.

The process of checking passenger tickets was well tried and tested. The guard would work a few paces ahead of the ticket inspector opening the compartment doors loudly to rouse any dozing passengers. Then he would ask them loudly to have tickets ready for inspection, before moving forward to the next compartment and so on. Meanwhile, the ticket inspector would be examining and clipping the tickets that had been produced ready.

Working together it would normally take perhaps forty-five minutes to do a full check. But tonight, there were very few passengers and the guard, accompanied by the ticket inspector, got to the last carriage before the guard's brake very quickly indeed. Inside the brake, a team of robbers was only part way through their work.

The guard, who was a few paces ahead of his colleague, noticed a man he later recognised (after the GTR and photographs of all the offenders appeared in the national press) as Jimmy White.

The guard believes that White was keeping lookout, ready to summon help and prevent the work of his associates in the guard's brake being interrupted.

White told the railway men that his ticket was with his friends in the last compartment (next to the guard's brake) and Guard Owen accepted that and continued to work the final coach. Meanwhile in the dining car, a soldier was explaining to Len Tappy, the senior steward, he had been wrongly advised at Euston and would be in real trouble as a result. He was on the wrong train and would be hopelessly late back to his barracks. 'Could you get the train stopped at Crewe?' he asked.

Len wanted to help but the only way he could was by introducing the young soldier to Guard Owen who might be able to arrange for a special stop. Len explained to the young soldier and they set off together to find the guard.

When Guard Owen reached the final carriage, he threw the door open and called to the several male occupants to have their tickets ready. The guard describes these men as all very well dressed, and some were holding up newspapers and magazines.

Guard Owen then turned towards the locked door giving access to his brake. As he did so one of the last passengers referred to (Guard Owen later identified the man as Bruce Reynolds) shuffled out into the corridor as if searching for his ticket. The guard moved to the connecting door to the brake, while Tom, the ticket collector, moved slightly into the compartment to examine the tickets of Reynolds' accomplices.

Reynolds moved behind the ticket collector and pushed him in the back. The ticket collector tripped over the outstretched feet of the seated robbers and onto the floor. There he was set upon with coshes. Guard Owen was immediately attacked too, and again coshed to the floor. The guard later identified Roy James (another convicted train robber) as being amongst those who attacked them.

Ticket Inspector Tom Thomas had a significant gash inflicted to his head and it immediately began to bleed profusely; both men suffered significant injuries. They were dragged, semi-conscious and covered in blood, into the guard's brake.

All around them other robbers were still at work ripping open high-value mailbags.

Bleeding and defeated, they were forced face down onto the mailbags, bound at the wrists and ankles with 'nylons' and warned to keep quiet. One of the robbers threatened that he had a gun and would use it unless they remained silent. A few minutes later Len Tappy and the soldier arrived and entered the guard's brake. They were immediately attacked and repeatedly coshed about the head. Both put up a significant defence, but they were too greatly outnumbered. Now the robbers had four bodies to mind, four more than they expected.

Tommy Thomas, another of the buffet stewards, was next – he got the same treatment. This left only the young steward Michael Carey minding the dining car.

Eventually, Michael wandered down the train looking into every compartment and lavatory wondering where all his colleagues could have gone. Then he reached the guard's brake. He tried the handle and it was locked. There was nowhere else his colleagues could be. He called out to them asking if they were in there and whether everything was alright. Then came the most stupid reply: 'It's alright, it's the police, now fuck off.'

Young Michael seems to have believed that policemen would never use such language! So for the wrong reason he reached the right conclusion and pulled the emergency cord. The train's brakes were immediately applied, and the train screeched to a halt. Fortunately for the robbers they came to a stop at Hemel Hempstead Station.

Now, if the cord had been pulled just a few minutes earlier, the train would have stopped in isolated farmland in freezing conditions and several feet of snow. The robbers, without communications or the means to get very far, in complete darkness, totally inappropriately dressed and without lighting or compass, would have been hopelessly lost and immediately vulnerable. But that is not what happened.

Roger Cordrey and another member of the gang had driven further up the line to the other side of Hemel Hempstead near Tring. There the two robbers had set about preparing to alter one signal to yellow and the other to red. Then as planned, they drove to a nearby telephone kiosk and awaited the call to confirm the exact timing of the train.

This was a very significant part of the plan because it was vital that the timing of the change of signals was accurately done. If Roger acted too early, then he might stop a preceding train. If he had, then the driver of the wrong train (or his Second Man) would have alighted and warned the signalman by means of the emergency phone at the red signal, that a false red signal was being shown. Once the signalman had received such an emergency call he would, in order to prevent the possibility of a collision, have stopped the 'target train' that was following behind a few miles away. Alternatively, if the phone call to the signal box had failed, the target train could have ploughed at high speed into the rear of the stationary one. It would be an almighty foul-up either way. To prevent this happening, the Raiders always made sure that the target train was on time and close to the right 'section' of track before altering signals.

The method of ensuring that the train was on time was simple. A getaway vehicle would park at or near the nearest railway station and watch for the train. Once the train was spotted, they would ring the call box where Roger awaited.

On that night in February 1963, six months before the GTR, two getaway cars waited near Hemel Hempstead Station. But the drivers didn't see the Irish Mail pass through at speed and on time. Instead they saw the train come to a stop. They saw the mail van doors being thrown open and their accomplices jump from the train and make a desperate dash to escape before the police could be summoned.

Tom Wisbey recollected that there were about eight robbers on the train that night, and this number has been generally reported before. But in addition, there were two robbers at the signals and another two driving the getaway cars. So, at least twelve train robbers were involved in the 'Irish Mail' job. What was the total value of goods stolen? I have seen it reported as about £3,000 and in those days that was enough to pay three hardworking men for more than a year. But for professional robbers like these, it was no more than 'beer money'. It is hard to believe that a gang of at least twelve gangsters would put themselves to such trouble without the promise of a small fortune. Unless…

As Cook discovered during his research, C11 and certain Flying Squad officers were also, at this time (February 1963) beginning to pick up word that a 'big job' was being planned by a specially assembled gang. Other than that, they had little to go on and resolved to keep their ears to the ground. As bold, calculating and successful as this raid was, sceptics at Scotland Yard doubted that this was the 'big job' that was apparently in the offing.[*]

There is only one reasonable explanation. This was a rehearsal. There were so many robbers involved that night not because the job required it, but because Mr Big had just combined two criminal gangs and was determined that these men would practise working together.

Tom Wisbey admitted to me his part in this crime, though none of the Great Train Robbers had ever been charged with it. But of course he only did so on the basis that we were writing fiction (see appendices).

A night attack on a mail train carrying high-value mails, the violent use of the cosh against rail staff, the threat of the use of guns, a train travelling on the Euston Line in the Tring area, the presence of the South Coast Raiders plus Reynolds, White, James and others. Does this sound familiar to anyone else?

It is said that British Transport Police HQ officers visited Holyhead the following day to take statements. A week or so later, Howel Owen and Tom Thomas were given the opportunity to make a formal identification of suspects but were unable to do so. The names of the suspects that were shown to those witnesses is not now known. Neither is it clear what was stolen, although newspaper accounts claim various numbers of mail packages were taken; some mention diamonds whilst other accounts say it was cash. In any event, what is indisputable is that that crime was very poorly executed and could easily have led to the arrest or even death of those who became Great Train Robbers.

---

[*] Cook, *The Untold Story*.

The information above is taken from the account provided by the guard of the train that night, Howel Owen (as shown in the excellent book *The Forgotten Train Robbery*, written by Mr Owen's son, Arwel). His account was substantially corroborated by Tom Wisbey and supported by press and official records at the time.

Gordon Goody in *How to Rob a Train* says, 'the first whisper of the Great Train Robbery came in May 1963.' Why would he say that if it weren't true? Perhaps it was because Goody was never charged with participating in the Irish Mail train robbery and was, therefore, notionally still liable to arrest and trial. Perhaps it was because the truth points to a wider conspiracy. As you will see, his account of what happened during May, June and July that year is both fundamental to the case against an innocent man and provably false.

THIRTEEN

BRITISH RAILWAYS' RESPONSE

Imagine the scene on the day after the Great Train Robbery. The Post Office chiefs are furious that this could ever occur. The Buckinghamshire Constabulary has a very major investigation on its hands and has had no experience of dealing with such people.

Suddenly, from the Home Secretary to the Met Commissioner, from there to the Assistant Commissioner (Crime) and on down to the operational detectives, all are put under pressure to get immediate results. The Flying Squad is ordered to take charge and bring the offenders to justice with a minimum of delay.

British Railways looks incompetent (again).

The Establishment view is clear: crime must most definitely be shown not to pay. The atrocious train robbery is a crime against the State.

Questions are being asked in the House of Commons and the Home Secretary, the Postmaster General and the Minister of Transport all have not only egg but a whole 'full English' on their chubby faces. The newspapers are full of it, and the whole nation is asking, 'How could this possibly happen?'

You can imagine the size of the shovels being used to shift the blame. No doubt the positioning was something like:

'Not the Home Secretary's responsibility, this is a matter for the Ministry of Transport and the Postmaster General, although we will of course do whatever is needed to help the responsible authorities.'

'Not the Post Master General's fault. Sadly, it was because BR failed to create proper security arrangements and failed to properly maintain the "high security" TPO coaches. In addition BR failed to respond quickly enough when the TPO came to an unscheduled stop.'

'Not British Railways' fault. No one should blame British Railways. We did all we were contractually obliged to do. This was essentially a Post Office train running on British Railways lines. We provided a locomotive, a guard, a driver and Second Man. It is widely known that our staff did all they could.'

That's pretty much how it seems to have gone. But below that sort of public positioning you can imagine British Railways must have been extremely keen to get to the truth of it all. After all, it could happen again. You can imagine the Home Secretary quietly pressing the Met Police Commissioner to get the Flying Squad to sort it out pronto, before others thought they could also take on the State and win. As for the Post Office, behind the scenes they must have been febrile in their efforts to show how BR had let them down.

But the truth, certainly so far as British Railways is concerned, is surprisingly different. There is absolute proof that at the most senior level of British Railways, the reaction was one of contempt. Over twenty years after the robbery, the man who was BR's Chief Operating Officer at the time of the robbery wrote:

> It is always fun – or nearly always – when Institutions and the Establishment … fall into derision. And if someone had not knocked the engineman of the Up Postal about quite badly the whole of the Great Train Robbery would have been good clean fun. Even as it was, my part in it was fun.
>
> As Chief Operating Officer I fell into derision because the whole thing was my fault. It began quietly enough. The telephone by my bed purred me awake.

Fiennes, the most senior operations man on the railway then describes the banter between himself and the railways control-room staff who had telephoned him in the early morning just hours after the robbery. Having been told about it all, he tells us in his book that he responded, 'Gone have they?' and laughed.

He goes on:

It was clearly a highlight in railway history, but at that moment, which was after Euston had cleared the (railway) line, it seemed a business for the police and the Post Office rather than BR and it seemed secondly, that (I) might be in the game but rather like a touch judge, running about and waving a flag at people who had committed offences. If anyone was tearing their hair, it should have been my friend Brigadier Kenneth Holmes, the Director of Postal Services, who owned and staffed travelling post offices. This (My) sense of well-being like that after a dose of phosgene gas lasted a few hours.'

The entertaining Mr Fiennes continues:

(Later that same day) people tried to convince me it was no laughing matter and secondly that it was my fault. 'They got away with two-and-a-half-million pounds' they said *avec empressement*, not realising that the sum took the whole affair higher into the cloud cuckoo land of laughter. *

---

* Gerard Fiennes, *Fiennes on Rails: Fifty Years of Railways*.

FOURTEEN

THE SIGNALS AND TRAIN CREW

I mentioned earlier that in 1981, I had full access to the Met Police Great Train Robbery file. I also told you that it was about a cubic yard of papers. The witness statements alone numbered more than 2,300. As you can imagine, I had no need or inclination to read every page. I concentrated on looking for connections between convicted and suspected Great Train Robbers and their associates in order to help me in the crime I was investigating.

I did not read all the statements by the TPO staff for instance, or those from railwaymen who attended the scene, or the junior and more senior police officers who had major or minor roles. Nor did I read the statements made to the police by Driver Mills, or his Second Man (David Whitby), or the signalman on duty at Leighton Buzzard signal box (Mr Wyn-De-Bank) or at Cheddington signal box (between which the robbery occurred).

The significance of the actions and inaction of the man on duty at the key signal box at Leighton Buzzard on the night of the robbery seems to have remained similarly unappreciated by the police, the courts and those who have written about the robbery ever since.

Firstly, what should the signalman on duty that night have done when he became aware that a green signal had unaccountably changed?

Well the *British Railways Rule Book* (1950 edition), provides the necessary instructions for all signalmen, train drivers, guards and firemen (driver's assistant or 'second man'). Long experience had taught the railway authorities the clear danger of disaster when signals fail and trains stop suddenly. The longer they remain stationary, the greater the danger, especially when the phones have also failed and train staff remain incommunicado.

The regulations are therefore lengthy, thorough and mandatory. They emphasise the need for the guard to take immediate action to 'protect' the train. He must do this by communicating with the driver and laying detonators at particular distances apart up to a total distance of one mile behind the train and ahead of it. Such detonators will explode if crushed by an approaching train. The second train is thus warned to stop.

The driver of the train that has stopped at an unexpected red signal is instructed to wait two minutes, then have the second man, or guard, use the signal telephone to speak with the signalman. The signalman will obviously need to immediately stop any further trains entering that section and call assistance as necessary. He must also communicate with the signalman at the next box ahead of the train. If the delay continues, the signalman is required to stop the next train passing in the direction of the stationary train and ask the driver to proceed at a slow speed to establish what has taken place.

The signalman responsible for the section on which the train has stopped has the fullest duties. He must report immediately any signal failure, or irregularity, in order for an examination and repairs to be carried out without delay. Clearly this needs to be done urgently for safety purposes and so that the movement of trains can be reinstated. He must 'protect' the stationary train by stopping others from speeding towards it. And he must enquire as to why the train is stationary. He cannot do that by simply leaving his signal box and walking to where the train is; he must rather call out assistance with a minimum of delay (obviously).

You might think that since the signalman, Wyn-De-Bank, knew that a very high-value TPO had been stopped inexplicably that night in 1963, he would have been particularly anxious to ensure that nothing had gone wrong. You might think that once he became aware that the signals were playing up and the TPO had made an unscheduled stop, he would react quickly. And if you were at the subsequent trial of the robbers, you might think that he and the other railway staff had done a pretty good job, excellent in fact. The truth is much murkier and suspicious.

Fortunately, during the course of research, I found a copy of the BR Internal Enquiry Report on the very issue of how the rail staff responded that night. I must admit I quickly assumed that no one else had a copy, because it seemed to me that no one has previously published or broadcast its contents. But, surprisingly, I have since discovered that at least two other copies have been in the public domain for years. A Mr Anthony Glazebrook, a former BR executive has a copy and apparently wrote about it in *The Times* a few years ago (he tells me). In addition I have recently had contact from Nigel Adams of Luton Model Railway Club. Mr Adams explained that several years ago he received a copy of these papers unexpectedly by post from Canada. Since that time he has used the papers to 'model' the train robbery scene for the benefit of the press and public who visit the club's train robbery crime scene model and the club's collection of related literature.

'My' copy of the BR papers was in the hands of the British Transport Police History Group and contained within a 2-inch thick file marked 'Great Train Robbery'. I didn't expect to find much. Most of it comprised old internal crime reporting details, just general stuff, and very little that wasn't mundane or could not be found in the newspapers of the day.

However, tucked away in the back of the folder was a pretty ordinary looking typed bundle of papers. It was headed: 'Memorandum of Joint Enquiry held at Euston on 12th August [1963]'. It contained formal written statements made by the key railway employees, details of their cross examination and a summary of evidence.

The internal railway enquiry focused on answering why the TPO stopped where it did and why the signalmen responded in the way they did. Remember, these statements were made before these witnesses had made statements to the police and when the

GTR had occurred little more than 72 hours earlier. The events were extremely recent and highly memorable.

We know that the TPO should have travelled at good speed on its journey from Rugby (its last stop) straight on to Euston. The signals should have been showing green all the way. The 'Up Postal Special' (train identity 1M44) had very high priority and was officially designated a 'class one service'.

However, as the train passed through Leighton Buzzard and into a section of track controlled by Leighton Buzzard No.1 Signal Box, Driver Mills and his Second Man saw an unexpected yellow dwarf signal (a dwarf signal is a low-level signal displayed at the side of the track).

Driver Mills applied the brakes and a red signal (known as the 'home signal' (a gantry signal) came into view. He slowed more and came to a stop at the gantry signal, several hundred yards from the signal box he had just passed. The signalman, Mr Wyn-De-Bank, told the enquiry that he saw the unexpected yellow signal but the 'red' (at the gantry) was not within his line of view. He said that as the train approached the 'red' it obscured his view of the 'yellow'.

Great Train Robbery Location
(Not to scale)

← South to London .... North to Rugby →

Bridego Bridge	Gantry Signals Sears Crossing	Dwarf Signals
Mails unloaded here	**Train hijacked here**	
↓	↓	↓

Down fast line ....
Up fast line ....
Down slow line ....
Up slow line ....

From Bridego Bridge →← to Cheddington Signal Box ← 2,870 yards (1.6 miles)	1,100 yards (2/3 of a mile)	→← From scene of attack on Driver Mills to Leighton Buzzard signal box 3,276 yards (1.9 miles) →

Driver Mills brought the train to a stop at 3.03 a.m., after which he and his Second Man were attacked. Then, under threat, Driver Mills took the locomotive and front two coaches a further 1,100 yards to Bridego Bridge (where the mailbags were stolen).

Of course, because the phone wires at the signals had been cut, neither Mills nor his colleague, Mr Whitby, could give information to the signalman. But remarkably, the record shows that the signal-box equipment indicated to the signalman that the train had been divided and the front portion had been moved forward to the site of the theft of the mailbags.

There are significant inconsistencies in Mr Wyn-De-Bank's evidence that are worthy of reflection. Mr Wyn-De-Bank, of course, knew that this train was a highly valuable and vulnerable TPO and that attacks on mail trains had been in the news. So why did he respond in the way he did? Read on. I have dissected each statement made to the enquiry to provide a timeline:

0250   Signalman Wyn-De-Bank in the Leighton Buzzard Signal Box 1 (north of the crime scene) says that the dwarf signal was showing a fault, a full three minutes before the TPO train approached his section.

0258   TPO passes Leighton Buzzard Signal Box heading south towards Cheddington on the fast line.

0258   Buzzer sounds immediately in the signal box warning that the dwarf signal (low-level signal next to track) has failed (the robbers had changed it). Signalman Wyn-De-Bank says he assumed that there was now no light whatsoever at this signal. He goes on, 'The yellow light re-appeared and the buzzer went again.'

He says he assumed that Driver Mills aboard the TPO would proceed slowly from the yellow light at the dwarf signal onwards to the gantry signal 1,387 yards further south (Sears Crossing) where he could use the phone at the signals to call him.

0300   Signalman Wyn-De-Bank says he phoned to get someone (a linesman called 'Mead') to come and check the line.

But later in evidence to the enquiry, Linesman Mead says he did
not receive the call until a full hour later. This is not necessarily
proof that the signalman was lying. Mr Wyn-De-Bank's phone
call was not made direct to Mr Mead and it is possible that the
intermediary delayed the call. However, given that the robbers
had calculated that they had only about thirty minutes to complete the attack, it is a vital issue. A delay in attracting railway
staff to the scene might well be judged as vital to the robbers and
much too important to be left to chance.

0307 or earlier   Signalman Kinchen at Cheddington signal
box is concerned at the lateness of the TPO and sees a parcel
train go past him on the 'Up' slow line heading towards
London, having just passed by the Leighton Buzzard signal
box. Signalman Kinchen thought it strange that the TPO
had not arrived first.

Importantly, later the driver of this parcel train stopped at Tring station and reported that he passed the TPO and saw it moving slowly
between Leighton Buzzard and Cheddington on the 'up fast'. This
is extremely important. It is a personal account of an independent
witness seeing the train approaching the false signals. More importantly it illustrates undoubtedly that Signalman Wyn-De-Bank had
the perfect opportunity to ask the parcel train driver to look out
as he passed by the stricken TPO and report his findings when he
arrived at the Cheddington Signal Box. Had he done so, the GTR
would most probably have been thwarted.

0308–0313   Signalman Wyn-De-Bank says that at about this
time he noticed that the instruments in the signal box indicated that the TPO had divided into two and that the front
portion had moved towards Bridge 127 (Bridego Bridge) in
the direction of Cheddington.

0308   According to the signalman at Cheddington, he called Mr Wyn-De-Bank at this time and enquired as to what had happened to the TPO. He would have expected it to pass by his signal box a few minutes earlier. At this stage, according to the Cheddington signalman, Wyn-De-Bank told him nothing at all about the TPO having divided; instead he said the train's lateness was due to signal failure.

0310   The Deputy Chief (Train) Controller at Euston said that at this time he was told that the TPO had not reached Tring: it was unaccountably late. He says that the TPO was a train that he 'kept his eye on'. This is a clear indication that the operational staff of the railways knew very well how vulnerable to attack the TPO was.

0315   Mr Wyn-De-Bank says that at this time he got a call from Cheddington Signal Box enquiring about the TPO. Note that this is a full seven minutes later than the time given by the Cheddington signalman.

0315–0319   Another call is received by Mr Wyn-De-Bank from the Cheddington signalman enquiring as to the whereabouts of the TPO.

0317   Another parcel train speeds past the scene on the 'down' fast line (heading north).

At this time yet another parcel train was heading south and would shortly approach the Leighton Buzzard Signal Box. Mr Wyn-De-Bank's statement says that he stopped this train and asked them to proceed slowly towards Cheddington and to try to establish what had happened to the TPO. This was quite a good thing for him to have done it seems, as it appears to show that he was, although belatedly, now keen for the truth to be quickly established. However:

0318   The Cheddington signalman told the story rather differently. He said that at this time he phoned Mr Wyn-De-Bank again and told him to stop the parcel train and get them to check the line.

0320   The Deputy Chief Controller at Euston phoned Wyn-De-Bank and asked what he knew. According to the statements, Signalman Wyn-De-Bank said little more than, 'It came past here!'

0328   The Deputy Chief Controller at Euston says he is aware that a parcel train has started the search between Leighton Buzzard and Cheddington.

If this is accurate, then the parcel train would have reached Bridego Bridge at about 0333, or almost exactly thirty minutes after the TPO was first attacked at Sears Crossing. A tight squeeze indeed.

0400   Linesman Mead says he was first alerted to report for duty and to inspect the line (by a call originating from Wyn-De-Bank).

0415   The parcel train that had been asked to conduct the search arrives at Cheddington Signal Box having stopped and picked up the injured Driver Mills, handcuffed to his Second Man, as well as the injured postmen. Police are called.

Under cross-examination of the witnesses several further interesting facts emerged:

1.   Signalman Wyn-De-Bank should not have been on duty that night but was there to replace the regular signalman who was on holiday.

2.   When asked under cross-examination, Mr Wyn-De-Bank stated that the buzzer (warning of a fault at the signal) had sounded in error several times prior to the night of the robbery. Yet when the supervisor responsible for the signal boxes was asked to confirm that this truly happened,

he told the enquiry, 'We have had no such reports from anyone and I would be very much surprised if it were true.'

3. When asked about what on earth he thought had happened to cause the TPO to be divided, Mr Wyn-De-Bank replied that he, 'thought it had been divided accidentally'.

There is clearly something very wrong about the signalman's evidence to the Enquiry.

The railway procedures, which are invariably followed because of the serious safety implications of not doing so, require:

a) The driver of the train to stop at the signals.

b) After a period of two minutes, the Second Man (assistant) to use the phone situated at the red light and confer with the signalman.

c) The signalman to advise the Second Man of the cause of the 'red'.

Yet, ten minutes after the train had stopped at the false signal, Mr Wyn-De-Bank had heard nothing and did nothing. He told no one. He said he knew the train had divided and then changed his mind – he didn't know it had divided.

It seemed to me that 'Wyn-De-Bank' was an unusual name and I might be able to trace his family. Within thirty-six hours I was speaking to the son of the now deceased signalman. He could not have been more helpful and honest. It was clear that he loved and respected his father, but nevertheless he told me:

Signalman Wyn-De-Bank had 'sailed close to the wind' from time to time.

Signalman Wyn-De-Bank had concealed from the railways, and everyone else, that prior to his BR employment he had served a period of time in HM Prison Bedford (bigamy).

Signalman Wyn-De-Bank, circa 1963.

A few years after the robbery a member of rail staff told Signalman Wyn-De-Bank's son that he suspected his father was involved in the robbery – months after the robbery, Signalman Wyn-De-Bank had bought his children brand new bikes. Not easy on a signalman's pay when bikes were the means by which most working men travelled.

Of course, you would expect the police to have picked up on all this at the time. Yet these are the exact and full words of Signalman Wyn-De-Bank's statement to the police, which clearly they accepted:

This witness THOMAS WILLIAM WYN-DE-BANK says

I live at 17 Railway Terrace, Bletchley. I am employed as a Railway Guard.

In August 1963 I was employed by British Railways as a Signalman.

On the night of the 7/8 August 1963 I was on duty at Leighton Buzzard No.1 Signal box at about 2.58 a.m. on the 8th August, 1963 the up postal train passed my signal box. At about 3 a.m. I received an indication by means of a buzzer that there was signal failure. It was on the up fast line and it could have been the distant or the home signal. It is the distant signal for the home signal at Sears Crossing. If one of the bulbs were taken out of one of the aspects of the distant signal it would raise the buzzer in my box. Due to the signal failure I expected to get a telephone call from the fireman of the train within a few minutes. I did not get a telephone call. About half an hour later I had an indication in my box that the up postal special had passed the home signal at Sears Crossing. At the same time my indicator showed that the up fast track to Sears Crossing was still occupied. I therefore assumed that part of the up postal train had been left behind at Sears Crossing.

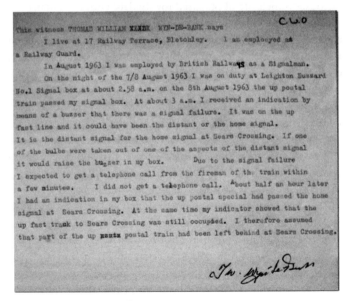

Signalman Wyn-De-Bank's court statement.

Obviously, this account differs substantially from the one given by him to the BR Enquiry. I can understand why the prosecutors would not want evidence to suggest that the signalman might be implicated; it does nothing to help prove the case against those charged and it is often the case that the prosecution will want to keep things simple so as not to confuse the jury. However, the statement reproduced in its entirety above not only contains important omissions but contains significant falsehoods.

For instance, we know very well that Mr Wyn-De-Bank earlier stated that he knew the dwarf signal had failed: he saw the yellow light where it should have been green. In his statement he says he thought the buzzer could have related to the distant or home signal. Further, we also know that he spotted that the train had divided more than fifteen minutes earlier than he later claimed.

Why was he so negligent? Why didn't he do his job? It seems to me there are only two possible reasons. Firstly, he might have willingly taken part in the robbery. If that is the case, then he was obviously hopelessly ill prepared for the BR enquiry. Then, once the enquiry was overcome, his only remaining hurdle would be to give evidence at the trial where his deceit might be uncovered. In any event, he was certainly aided in hiding the truth, wittingly or otherwise, by the British Railways drive to conceal any negligence on their part.

But surely if Signalman Wyn-De-Bank was part of the gang it would have made him a fortune? We all know that each of the robbers made enough for ten men to retire in luxury.

In truth it is rarely the case that all those involved in a complex crime get an even share ('whack'). Those who play a minor role, especially if coerced, would instead get a small sum (a 'drink' in the vernacular). Perhaps Signalman Wyn-De-Bank got to know one of the robbers, or their associates, whilst he was imprisoned? Or perhaps the robbers found out by other means that Mr Wyn-De-Bank 'had form' and could be coerced? He would surely be easy to win over; he and his family lived in a railway cottage – if someone had tipped off BR about his criminal conviction, he would potentially have lost both job and home.

Almost incredibly, during the course of the robbery, when at least fourteen men smashed their way onto the train, overpowered the three postmen working there and worked for about thirty minutes heaving mailbags from the train and down the embankment, scheduled trains passed the scene of the robbery as if nothing were amiss. Mr Wyn-De-Bank knew those trains were due. He alone had a duty to enquire about the TPO, yet he did nothing and told no one until pushed to do so by the signalman at Cheddington.

Did the robbers know that these trains would come along? Of course they did, and it was vital for the success of the robbery that the crew on those passing trains were not aware that something had gone wrong on the track.

A simple request to the driver of that first parcel train would have done it. Or if he had called his fellow signalman at Cheddington in reasonable time, the Cheddington signalman could also have stopped a north-bound passing train and made a similar request. Either signalman could then have asked a driver to move forward at cautionary speed, observe and report in to the next signal box.

Instead, Mr Wyn-De-Bank said that he phoned for a staff member to attend and walk the track to see what had happened. He said he did that at 0300. Odd that, because at that time the TPO hadn't actually stopped at the red light! The dwarf signal failed at 0258. Clearly, Mr Wyn-De-Bank was quick off the mark. But then again, the record shows, contrary to written instructions, he did not make a written entry showing that he called for the track to be inspected, let alone note the time the call took place. Remember, Linesman Mead says it happened an hour later.

According to the BR Enquiry:

Mr Wyn-De-Bank was closely questioned on his actions and the indicators he received on the signaling equipment. On being asked why he did not carry out the provisions of BR rule 16 when track circuit No.1 had been occupied for a considerable time, the signalman stated that he assumed that the I.B distant signal had not displayed any aspect as the train approached and the driver was approaching the home signal cautiously.

On being shown the train register book signalman Wyn-De-Bank <u>acknowledged that he had failed to record that the Kendall Parcels train had been stopped and cautioned</u> but he confirmed that he had stopped this train. When informed that the Euston /control office had recorded the failure of the I.B distant signal at 2.50 am, the signalman stated that he was certain that nothing had been revealed until the Postal had passed into the section.

Clearly the enquiry was very suspicious about Mr Wyn-De-Bank's evidence.

The enquiry staff wrote this final remark against all the evidence he had given. It also appears against every other witness:

<u>He had not been questioned by outsiders on railway signaling procedure.</u>

You might now be asking yourself, what on earth does that mean? Let me tell you: for 'outsiders' read 'the police'. It means that three days after the robbery these key witnesses were yet to be interviewed in any detail by the police. Judging by the brevity of the official police witness statement eventually made by Signalman Wyn-De-Bank, they never were.

It might be that you see the motivation for this, but for the sake of those who don't know the difference between the 'four foot' and a station platform, let me just explain a little. Internal railway enquiries of the past were not designed to serve the public good. They were there to allow the railways to orchestrate the evidence of witnesses to significant events so as to minimise the risk of litigation against the railways and preserve the best possible image. Sometimes that included making hurried changes to railway procedures and the quick tightening up of safety issues.

The sceptical amongst you might be asking, 'How can he know that?' My answer is that after thirty-one years as a railway detective and having fought Railtrack and Great Western trains following the Southall Train Crash, I know exactly how the system worked. Those organisations fought hard, by every means possible, to further their self-interest. It was for that reason that following the Southall train crash, and in spite of pressure from Railtrack, Great Western trains, the Department of Transport and my own bosses, I refused to release evidence to a railway enquiry before that evidence had been considered by the courts.

You might be surprised if you were to read public comments by British Rail about Signalman Wyn-De-Bank's performance that night. He is described as 'diligent', and there is no hint of error or omission on his part. Their very clear suspicions are kept secret.

Of course, errors and omissions and cover-ups do not in themselves prove an individual's criminal guilt. Mr Wyn-De-Bank deserves to be treated as innocent, what I have discovered does not amount to conclusive proof of criminality. But what does most certainly exist are circumstances and events that should have demanded that 'outsiders' (the police) paid close attention to Mr Wyn-De-Bank's actions, errors and omissions that night.

The Great Train Robbery investigation was conducted under the leadership of the Metropolitan Police Flying squad. They focused on providing leadership, coordination and taking a lead on the analysis of current criminal intelligence and specific targeting of informants, as well as the forensic science element. Many other agencies were involved, but for current purposes let me say the British Transport Police took the lead on all internal railway enquiries and statements from railway staff such as the signalmen. Their other role was to look for a potential 'insider' from within the railways who might have provided information to the robbers.

One big final point on the issue of how on earth the robbers could have known that the TPO was so well loaded. The obvious conclusion was that one or more people phoned them on the night upon the train's departure at Glasgow and again as it travelled south picking up more bags.

That is a pretty obvious and no doubt accurate description of what took place. Therefore, the police and Post Office, to identify any suspect trunk calls en route, extensively researched all telephone calls at GPO exchanges. In those days if you wanted to phone a different part of the country you had to go via your local GPO telephone exchange operator and all such calls were logged.

But how many of those Met and county police officers would have been aware that the railways had a remarkable internal national phone system in operation even then? Every BR station department, every signal box and thousands of other railway premises had twenty-four-hour access to this private national phone system. Any staff member at any location could 'direct dial' any other railway number anywhere in the country, or via the twenty-four-hour BR operator could request and be given an 'external line' to ring any GPO number anywhere. Yet, I have seen or heard nothing to suggest that anyone involved in the Great Train Robbery investigation, or anyone writing about it since, has ever considered this a potential means by which the robbers could have been updated on the night.

The fact that the robbers were notified that there was a heavy load that night, in excess of a hundred bags, came from an informant within a couple of weeks of the robbery. The tally of bags did not reach 100 until the train reached Tamworth at 1.23 a.m. By that time, it is commonly accepted that Gordon Goody, who apparently received the call, was well ensconced at Leatherslade Farm and out of reach.

Before arriving at Crewe, where Driver Mills took over the train, there were still only ninety-one high-value mailbags loaded, and that was well after midnight. Yet it remains that Goody seems to have been sure before the gang left Leatherslade Farm that night, that there were more.

What we do know is that Goody and gang anticipated a truly exceptional payday. They must have received information from someone (or more) who had observed the TPO that night as it made its way south. This clearly points, as the Post Office investigators concluded, to someone on the train that night providing information. But the alternative answer is that a number of individuals observed from platforms when the train stopped en route to load more mailbags. An accessible phone system would have been vital.

Train guard Miller was 61 years old at the time of the robbery and had been a railwayman for over forty years. On that fateful night he boarded the TPO at Carlisle, no doubt thinking it would be a routine trip all the way to Euston. The statement he made to the BR enquiry is hardly credible. After I first read the account I felt a bit sorry for him. I assumed he had been asleep on the job, woke suddenly, panicked and then did his hopeless best.

He is another railway staff witness who has been largely overlooked, but whose testimony at the BR internal enquiry is worth looking at closely. His statement shows all was normal until the train came to a stop at Sears Crossing gantry signal. He says he saw the signal was red and 'turned around' and 'watched my vacuum gauge needle go down to zero'. This of course was as a result of the robbers disconnecting the front of the train from the remainder. It meant the train could not move. The guard says he immediately climbed from the guard's brake onto the track, made his way forward and climbed back on to speak to the Post Office supervisor (there was no direct access from the guard's brake to the TPO). After speaking with the supervisor, the guard got off the train at the sixth carriage from the front. He says that at that point he 'saw the two leading carriages and the engine had disappeared'.

Can you imagine? He must have wondered what on earth had happened. He says he had a look at the couplings and vacuum pipe, then, in accordance with Rule 179, walked back towards the signal box for a distance of one mile. Rule 179 required him to 'protect' the train by placing detonators on the line to warn any approaching trains. Remember the rule described earlier in the context of the driver's responsibility? Well the guard also has a duty to report to the signalman.

It is important here to know the distances between the key locations (see page 144). From Mr Wyn-De-Bank's signal box to the false red signal (the place at which the train was divided) it was just over 3,200 yards (about 1.9 miles). From that point to Bridego Bridge where the mailbags were unloaded was 1,100 yards (about 0.7 of a mile).

Oddly, Guard Miller told the enquiry that he walked the pre-scribed mile away from the train (towards the dwarf signal), then another mile all the way back to the scene. At that point accord-ing to his evidence, he approached the signal phone. On trying to call the signal box he found the wires on the signal post tel-ephone had been cut.

According to his own testament, Guard Miller decided he would next walk to Cheddington signal box, nearly three miles south (passing Bridego Bridge therefore). He claims to have placed three more detonators in front of the abandoned carriages before setting off.

Now remember, this was a clear, warm summer night. The weather was fine and there was moonlight. It would be quiet but for the noise of any train. The guard, who had a clear line of sight to the scene of the robbery, says that he saw and heard nothing right up to the moment that he actually arrived at the scene of the ransacked mail coaches.

Guard Miller then reports that he stopped a freight train and reported what had happened.

As you would expect, Guard Miller was asked some impor-tant questions during the BR Enquiry. In cross-examination he stated that after his train stopped at Sears Crossing (at the false red signal) at 3.03 a.m. he saw the needle drop on the gauge (caused by the train being separated) at 3.05 a.m. He says it took him about four minutes from the time he noticed the vacuum being lost to climb from the his brake, speak to the postmen and walk to the front, at which point he could see that the locomotive and part of the train was missing.

How could the following have been accomplished in four minutes?

- Second Man Whitby climbs down from the cab, goes to the signal phone and finds it not working. He approaches someone he sees back down the track behind the locomotive and two lead coaches. He is attacked and pushed down the embankment.

- Robbers then uncouple the engine and two leading coaches. This would have taken both skill and strength. The couplings (known as buck-eyes) weigh over 50kg and would have had to be manipulated in the dark with the train connections in the way. Having done that, the robbers then had to disconnect the vacuum-brake pipes and other connections and re-couple the vacuum pipe onto what would become the front portion of the train. It would have been a time-consuming process (and one of the reasons why the railways were in the process of fitting air brakes which are much easier and faster to attach and detach). All this would have taken at least ten minutes at the absolute minimum.

- Robbers take part in the struggle with Driver Mills and he is seriously injured.

- Second Man Whitby is brought back to the locomotive and with Driver Mills, placed in the engine room at the back of the driving cab.

- The robbers' train driver climbs aboard and makes various efforts to move the train.

- Driver Mills is brought back to the driver's cab and is persuaded to move the train as directed. He has to recreate the vacuum to release the brakes (two or three minutes).

- The front portion of the train moves forward and out of view.

All this in about four minutes? Either the guard was completely hopeless and had no idea of time, or things did not happen in the way we have all believed.

However, we can say for certain that at least some of his timings are accurate. He said the train stopped at Sears Crossing at 3.03 a.m. That appears to be true. He says at 3.07 he walked for two miles on loose ballast (walking north for one mile and back for one mile). If we say he managed to walk at about three miles an hour (a reasonably fast pace) he would be back at the train at about 03.47.

He told the enquiry that he tried to use the signal phone and found the wires cut before starting his trek towards Bridego Bridge placing detonators as he went. At the same pace his walk to the scene at Bridego Bridge would have taken him about fifteen minutes. He would have arrived there shortly after 4 a.m., and that fits well with the evidence of others who met him there.

You might think that the guard could not have done all of the above in less than an hour. The problem is this: the more time we allocate for his completion of those tasks, the less time we can allow for all that others allege occurred in the attack on the locomotive and the division of the train. Something seems to be wrong.

The story of Driver Mills is a tragic one. After the attack that night, he was clearly a broken man. He apparently suffered from headaches for the rest of his shortened life. Once apparently a strong, independent man, a loving husband to Florence and father to his children, after the raid his life changed irretrievably. Seven years later he died of leukaemia. You would have to have a very hard heart indeed not to be touched by the tragedy that his life, and that of his family, became from the moment of injury until his premature death.

The accepted story is that Driver Mills was attacked by 'someone with an iron bar wrapped in a cloth'. Mills was apparently fighting off one robber when, 'Suddenly he was struck on the head from behind … (He) sank to his knees, his face covered in blood'.[*] However, many years later, the story is told somewhat differently.

Fordham says that Driver Mills confided in her, years after the event, on the understanding that she would never repeat his words. She says she stuck to that arrangement until after his death. Apparently, Driver Mills revealed to her that the assault only caused a superficial scalp wound that bled profusely, but the serious injury was caused when he struck his head when falling.

---

[*] Fordham, *The Robbers' Tale*, p.64.

Fordham says she asked Mr Mills two questions: was it true that he had told a reporter earlier that the robbers had treated him like a gentleman? And secondly, why did he not tell the court how his injuries were actually caused? Fordham says Mr Mills became very agitated. After all, if the court had been given this account of the attack it might well have caused a reduction in prison sentences. Apparently, Driver Mills begged Fordham not to repeat this account because he had been told that if this truth were told then his railway pension would be affected.

Does any of that have the ring of truth? Well, it is certainly possible that Mr Mills' injury was caused in the way now described. We know the Establishment was extremely keen to paint the robbers in the worst possible light. We know there was also a sort of panic about the crime. For instance, almost unbelievably, Sir Alec Muir, the Chief Constable of Durham, after the robbers had been locked away, wrote that he feared there would be a prison break involving the use of tanks and/or the use of nuclear weapons. So fearful was he of the robbers that he suggested they should all be quietly 'eliminated'.**

So, is it possible that Driver Mills was pressured by the authorities into misleading the court? Could the fact that Mr Mills might have felt partly responsible for the extra-long sentences imposed have affected his mental well-being thereafter? Could it be that the burden of knowing that he had misled the court weighed heavily on his shoulders? Could the threat of the removal, or reduction, of his railway pension have been the sort of blackmail to torment him forever?

If the answer to those questions is 'Yes', then you are left asking, 'Did the powers that pushed him to give an inaccurate account of the attack and threatened his pension do him greater harm than those who struck him? Of course, none of that detracts from the probability that Mr Mills was an entirely innocent man who acted bravely that night. But it does leave me, and I do hesitate to say this, wondering what actually happened.

** *The Sun*, 27 February 1969.

Is there any other potential interpretation of events, unpalatable as they might be? Well, I hate to say it, but if we look at things objectively, there clearly is.

Whilst researching for this book I found it difficult to find out anything about the other train driver, 'Pop' or 'Peter'.

Remember, Ronnie Biggs allegedly recruited him. It is commonly accepted that Biggs persuaded Bruce Reynolds that 'Pop' could move the TPO to Bridego Bridge once the driver (Mills) had been removed. The story goes that when it came to it, 'Pop' tried in vain to move the train but couldn't manage it. They say they had to get Driver Mills back on the 'footplate' to do the job. But why is it that 'Pop' (aka Alf, Old Alf, Stan or Peter) largely disappears from accounts given by the robbers as soon as he is ejected from the locomotive?

It is true that Gordon Goody describes a van with a false bottom turning up at Leatherslade Farm and that Pop's share was loaded into it, but it is simply an aside. When you read detailed accounts, even the highly imaginable one of Reynolds, there is little mention of this mysterious train driver.

Of course, many years later, people claimed to have found the man concerned. Again, much later the well-known liar Ronnie Biggs introduced the name 'Stan Agate'. But if you suspend belief in 'Pop', 'Peter', Stan' etc. and imagine that there was no replacement train driver, what then? What if Driver Mills was only supposed to be 'dusted up', given a few punches to convince the authorities? What if, dare I say it, the serious injury was caused as he later said it was (accidentally) and he had agreed long before that he would move the train to Bridego Bridge?

Why in the BR Enquiry papers is there no mention by Second Man Whitby or Driver Mills of the robbers' engine driver 'Pop'? Obviously, 'Pop' must have been there and made his failed attempts to drive before Driver Mills was reinstated. Why didn't the Second Man hear the row between the robbers and 'Pop' as their frustration boiled over? There are two possible explanations. Firstly, 'Pop' made his attempt to drive the train forward while Mr Whitby was delayed on the embankment by the robbers. The other explanation is that 'Pop' never existed.

This year (2019), out of the blue I received a message from a retired railway employee from the Bletchley area. He said that years ago he had been quietly told that Driver Mills was the sort of man who never swapped his hours of duty. Whatever he was rostered to do, he did. Yet on the night of the robbery, this man from Bletchley told me, he had swapped duties to drive the TPO.

He also gave me a character description of Driver Mills. It was one that I have never seen or heard before.

Weeks later, I was speaking with a long-since-retired train driver who many years since moved away from Crewe and knew of Mills. He gave me the same character description. I am left wondering, if the first caller from Bletchley was able to give an accurate character description of Mills, is it possible that his other revelation, about Mills swapping his duties, is also correct? I have been unable to find out.

I have tried to find evidence one way or the other but have found nothing to confirm or deny it. What we do know is that the train could have been stationary at Sears Crossing signals for no more than a few minutes.

Driver Mills – I have his BR enquiry statement in front of me – puts it this way:

> I saw two men come towards the Second Man and another man began to climb into the cab. I thought they were P-Way staff but when they came into the light of the cab I noticed they were masked. I grappled with this man and then I was hit from behind by another man, who had entered the cab from the opposite side. Under the impact of these blows I sank to the ground and was overpowered.

Note he says he 'sank to the ground'. He doesn't say he fell and bashed his head. So was he misleading the enquiry and later the police and then the court? The alternative is that Driver Mills was not being accurate when he 'confessed' to Fordham, or that Fordham is 'mistaken' when she says Mills made a confession to her.

I don't know the answers to the questions raised above, but they are real questions that have not, it seems, been raised before. Or so I thought until 29 April 2019. On that day I heard from another old colleague. He must be well into his eighties now. A former army sergeant, he became a well-respected police sergeant and was serving in the BTP at the time of the robbery. He told me that it was a whispered rumour in 1963, within BTP circles at the time, that Driver Mills was 'involved in the robbery'. That is not proof, and if every rumour or allegation were true then I would myself by now have served a substantial period of my life in prison. But nevertheless, there it is.

On a lighter note, during the course of researching into the immediate aftermath of the robbery, I was put in touch with former PC Gordon Blake. Gordon is in his eighties now and we had not spoken for over thirty years. He told me for the first time that he was on duty at Euston on the night of the robbery. I asked him if he remembered any information that night about Driver Mills, or Second Man Whitby, or how they were handcuffed etc.

He had no such detail in his head, but told me that it was always the case that the 'Up TPO' was met at Euston Station by at least two uniform constables. On the night in question, two calls came through from British Railways staff (probably the Euston Railway Control Centre). The first informed him that the TPO had been delayed (without explanation) and then at some time after 4 a.m. another call was received stating that it had been robbed. There was no information available at that stage about the treatment or handcuffing of the train crew.

But Gordon Blake did tell me that the Transport Police response was immediate, and part of that response was to ensure from that day, Transport Police officers escorted the TPO both on its 'Up' journey from Glasgow to London and on its return 'Down' trip to Glasgow.

That same day, PC Blake together with PC Frank Trevis, with just a couple of hours' break from their night duty, were dispatched, armed with wooden truncheons, to escort the TPO on its journey north. From that event, a pattern was quickly established and repeated with all TPOs across the country for thirty years.

The police-escorted London–Glasgow TPOs were code-named 'Paris' and 'Madrid', and every other one across the country was given a similar (country capital) title – Weymouth–London for instance was 'Zanzibar'. The Post Office Investigation Department did not participate.

Interestingly, PC Gordon Blake was also based at Euston at the time of both the earlier 'Irish Mail' robberies referred to previously and remembers the significant arrests that were made by Detective Inspector Kerr and his team (see Chapter 4).

FIFTEEN

THE ROBBERS THAT GOT AWAY

It was when Tom Wisbey stayed down in Hampshire to help me with the novel that he revealed the name Danny Pembroke. At first, Tom just gave me the name Danny, and he didn't confirm the surname until he had first checked with Danny's family that it was alright to do so. Of course, I asked Tom to tell me more about the character and habits of each of the robbers, and he seemed keen to tell me about his friend Danny. His affection and respect for Danny were obvious.

I wanted to know the small stuff for the novel we were doing – Did he smoke? What was his preferred drink? Was he a womaniser? Serious? Funny? Violent? A gambler? What car did he drive?

Danny Pembroke. Photo taken in about 1962.

Expressions? Background? Tom didn't really warm to the idea of telling me the intimate familiar things about him. But I could tell from the way he told me what he did that there was a good deal of affection for him.

He did tell me that Danny was a family man with children: the boy (now a man much my own age) was also called Danny and I believe there were two younger sisters too. The money Danny made was always for his family first. Yes, he liked to gamble and go 'to the horses and the dogs' but only in moderation. He didn't usually drink alcohol; his favourite drink was a mug of tea. He was a humble man from a poor background who, like Tom, saw crime as the only chance of getting any real money.

Apparently, he had a well-developed sense of humour and he and Tom would play silly tricks together on others. I remember Tom telling me how the two of them hid behind the front wall of someone's garden and how they tried to conceal their laughter as they threw lumps of soil/clay/mud at some unsuspecting official who was passing by, minding his own business. Apparently, he had no idea where the debris was coming from.

Tom made it plain that Danny was most definitely always the leader of the Raiders, no question. He told me, interestingly, about how when it came to a turf war, Tom had asked him about the extent of violence they should be prepared to use.

The advice that Danny gave him obviously stuck in Tom's head. 'It's just another job, we'll just do whatever we got to do to get the job done, no more than that.'

Of course Danny's advice to Tom didn't excuse the violence they both inflicted over the years, but it did show that they had at least applied their minds to the subject. You might think that makes matters worse. But it also shows that neither of them glorified or enjoyed that aspect of their work. Of course that only mitigates the violence used; it does not excuse it.

Danny Pembroke was named as a firm suspect within days of the robbery, though Detective Superintendent Butler, head of New Scotland Yard's Flying Squad, had him listed as *Dennis* Pembroke. It was a list cobbled together from known armed robbers, especially those who had robbed the Royal Mail, as well as information from formerly reliable informants.

After Tom's death, via Marilyn Wisbey, I tried to contact Danny's son (Danny).

I knew that Tom had his phone number. After all, Tom had contacted him to check whether it was alright to share information with me. But Marilyn could not find his number. I suspect that Tom had done what most of his profession did. All phone numbers were given a simple code and the names to which they referred altered too. For instance, one simple long-standing trick was to show the details of key contacts under their wives' Christian names. In any event, I have been unable to speak to Danny's son. However, at the time of writing this I am aware that Channel 4 have contacted him and he has corroborated the information that Tom Wisbey supplied to me.

At the time of the robbery Danny Pembroke lived near Tom at 22 Hood House, Elmington Estate, Camberwell, London SE5. The police had received information that one of the robbers was called 'Danny' and was a very close friend of Tom Wisbey and others suspected to have been involved. Butler must have wondered if this was Danny Pembroke or a Danny Regan. Both fitted the bill and both were brought in for questioning.

On 6 September, four weeks after the robbery, the Flying Squad paid Danny Pembroke a visit at his home. Of course, he denied everything. A search of the flat was conducted, but nothing was found. True to form, Danny had been careful. Nevertheless, Pembroke was arrested and taken to NSY for questioning by DCS Butler. It is an indication of how strongly they believed that Danny was involved that he was questioned by Butler in person.

According to Cook:

> In Butler's report to Commander Hatherill, he states that Pembroke was closely interrogated and denied complicity in the case. His palm prints were taken and compared with

several palm prints left at Leatherslade Farm by the robbers, but no identification was made.[*]

Later, once the full forensic examination of the farm had been completed, police had what they believed were samples of pubic hair from some of the robbers. Danny Pembroke consented to provide samples for comparison; once again the result was negative. With no forensic evidence against him, and with the only evidence being the uncorroborated word of an informer, the police had no choice. Pembroke was released.

Danny Regan, a bookmaker like his pal Tom Wisbey, was also closely interrogated and released. Clearly the Flying Squad could not be certain which 'Danny' was the guilty party.

A further police report indicates that Tom Wisbey's home, on the same estate as Danny's, was searched soon after. The report mentions in passing that as the officers carried out the search, Renee Wisbey (Tom's wife) made the officers tea. (And that is exactly how it happened in 1981 too.)

The information against Danny Pembroke was strengthened later when another police officer received similar information about a 'Danny' being involved, but this time the surname was attached. Nevertheless, no real evidence existed.[**]

Tom told me that a few years earlier, shortly before his death, Danny had confided in his old friend that he had always regretted not being captured with the rest of them. I guess the biggest and most audacious robbery of the twentieth century had conferred a sort of immortality on those named, and Danny was not then part of that number.

The Sansom brothers were Freddie, George and Terry. During the 1960s they were all well known to the police. They were again from South London although Terry Sansom's address was recorded by police as being Leighton Gardens, Kensal Rise, North West London.

---

[*]   Cook, *The Untold Story*.
[**] Cook, *The Untold Story*.

George and Terry were known associates of the Kray twins. Both were capable of extreme violence and demonstrated that during their chosen profession: armed robbery. Terry Sansom was acquitted of a robbery that took place in January 1961, involving the theft of a £9,400 payroll. During the crime a security guard, James Hawney, was murdered.

Although charged with murder, Terry Sansom was acquitted on that charge too. Like Tom Wisbey in later life, Terry was charged with a significant drug offence. Unlike Tom Wisbey, he was again acquitted.

Because Terry had been an occasional member of the South Coast Raiders, he was a known associate of Tom Wisbey and Danny Pembroke. It was no surprise therefore that Terry and George's names, both known Post Office robbers, were prime suspects after the Great Train Robbery. Newspaper reports later suggested that one of the brothers was the unknown 'Mr Three', but while both brothers fitted the bill, the newspaper talk was mere speculation.

As stated earlier, two of the Sansom brothers were included on a list of GTR suspects compiled by Detective Chief Superintendent Tommy Butler, head of the Flying Squad. It was with that in mind that I raised the issue with Tom Wisbey. I knew the Sansom family was well known to him. I knew from the files I read many years ago that when Tom's daughter Lorraine was tragically killed in a car crash, the car in which she travelled was owned by one of the Sansom family, the boyfriend of Lorraine's sister, Marilyn.

I remember in the early 1980s reading about the Sansoms in the Met Police Great Train Robbery file. I distinctly recall that in describing that car crash, a gold-coloured Rolls-Royce was described. How could I forget that story? How often do you read about a gold Rolls-Royce? I remember how ostentatious and therefore unwise it would be for the family of a suspected train robber to be flaunting their wealth in that way. It was only whilst researching for this book and checking facts with Marilyn Wisbey that I found out the police intelligence report was wrong.

There never was a gold Rolls-Royce, though the police report was otherwise accurate.

So, in 2015, when I asked Tom if it was George or Terry Sansom who had been a fellow robber on the GTR, Tom surprised me. He shook his head, thought for a moment and said, 'Try Freddie'. He made it clear that it was Freddie Sansom who had taken part. He had no reason at all to lie and I believe he was telling the truth. So, who was this Freddie Sansom?

I have since found out that Freddie was the leader of a violent gang of bank robbers known as the 'Shot in the Ceiling Gang'. They would announce their arrival at the target bank, and get the attention of staff and customers alike, by discharging a sawn-off shotgun into the ceiling. Freddie was a close associate of the Krays and a neighbour of Jim Hussey. He was friendly with Tom, of course, and the rest of the Raiders, but also well known to Mad Frankie Frazer and the rest of the London 'faces' of the day.

For whatever reason, the lists of suspects compiled at New Scotland Yard included two of the Sansom brothers, while the name of the third brother, Freddie, the one who was actually involved in the Great Train Robbery, does not appear. I wonder why that was?

In August 2019, I made contact with Kenny Sansom, the retired international footballer, and told him what I had concluded about his Uncle Fred. He agreed that the police had wrongly suspected his father and other uncle; Freddie was the one they should have focused on.

I later received a phone call from Freddie's sister, Pat. She has asked me to make it plain that she does not believe her older brother Freddie was part of the Great Train Robbery Gang but could offer no explanation as to why Tom Wisbey would wrongly implicate her brother.

SIXTEEN

THE TRUE INSIDER

The 2016 book *The Curse of the Great Train Robbery* states: 'It was Field who had started the ball rolling when he introduced Patrick McKenna, the Ulsterman, and at the very least, he (McKenna) should have served a lengthy prison sentence for conspiracy.'* So, it seems to be positively concluded: McKenna was the key insider who became known as the Ulsterman, the matter apparently settled in history. But what a gross error it is. Where did it all start?

The day after the Great Train Robbery the Postmaster General, The Right Honourable Reginald Bevin MP, was quoted in *The Times* as saying that the mail train raid 'may have been an inside job' and calling for a 'full and urgent enquiry'.**

A few months later, after the main criminal trial that she had witnessed, Peta Fordham concluded that a significant 'insider' had evaded detection. She was convinced that such person provided vital inside information about which train route would provide the richest pickings, such as what date would provide the most cash in transit and the best location en route to launch the attack. They could also, at short notice, advise on the need to delay the attack for twenty-four hours and keep the robbers abreast of progress of the train on the night in question.***

To those observations can be added that someone ensured that, for the first time, all three high-security TPO coaches were out of

---

*   Jon Fordham, *The Curse of the Great Train Robbery, p. 113.*
**   Russell-Pavier/Richards, *Crime of the Century*, p.45.
***   Fordham, *The Robbers' Tale*, p.36.

use, and perhaps that the forensic analysis of the locomotive and coaches would be disrupted.

After the Great Train Robbery occurred there was a massive outcry from all parts of the Establishment. The Postmaster General was in the firing line and extreme pressure must have been placed on the Post Office Investigation Department to find the Post Office insider.

Within three weeks of the robbery, a Mr R.F.Yates, a senior Post Office Investigation Department executive who sat with the senior-most police officers to pursue the investigation, concluded:

> I hold the view that meticulous planning would be undertaken by criminals of this calibre, that the arrangements would be precise and that, consequently, detailed information would be essential before embarking on such a venture. Furthermore, I think that provision would be made for any changes in procedure to be notified to the gang. Post Office employees in general would not, of course, be in a position to keep abreast of daily changes in TPO working, and the only officers apart from some of high rank or those employed in special security postal work who would be able to furnish impeccable information, are those actually employed on the Up and Down Special TPOs; those attached to the HQ of the TPO Section itself or those employed at railway stations in the loading and unloading of HVP mails from the Up Special TPO.*

The Post Office Investigation Department and the Transport Police apparently spent years trying to find out who it was that gave the vital inside information that made the Great Train Robbery possible. Yet their considerable combined forces never identified one good suspect.

It was years before Gordon Goody came up with the 'true identity' of 'The Ulsterman', the name adopted by the robbers for the postal worker concerned. Goody identified the Ulsterman as Patrick McKenna. On 28 September 2014, Goody's

---

* Cook, *The Untold Story*.

allegation was reported in *The Observer* newspaper although he had apparently earlier told the *Irish Times* that the Ulsterman was called Barry.**

By the time of Goody's death he had first called the Ulsterman 'Freddie' and then 'Barry' before settling on 'Mark McKenna'.

Since that item appeared in *The Observer*, in later books and umpteen articles and at least one video, 'The Ulsterman' Patrick McKenna has been promoted to 'The Mastermind'. Now, any quick Google search will reveal with assurance that Mr McKenna is undoubtedly the guilty party.

The first time I read about Goody's assertion about Mr McKenna, I knew in my bones that it was wrong. It was just another sordid attempt to make dishonest money – this time from an innocent man, or rather the reputation of a deceased man, unable therefore to defend himself.

For any impartial reader who cares to reflect, or check, on Goody's assertions, his account is easily falsified. For instance, Goody tells us that it has been discovered that:

> (McKenna) married a girl from Manchester at Islington Registry Office in 1949 at which time he (McKenna) lived at Southall Road, Beckenham, only ten minutes' walk from where we had the meeting at Finsbury Park. ***

Yet in reality Finsbury Park is in North London and an hour by tube and train from Beckenham in Kent, and nearly that long to reach by car. Why would Goody tell us all that Finsbury Park is ten minutes' walk from Beckenham? I can only think of three possible reasons: he had gone daft, or secondly, he thought we were all daft, or finally, he really didn't care so long as he was paid. There is a fourth possibility I suppose, that somewhere in his heart he felt it right to leave his lies to be easily exposed – after he had been paid for telling them!

** Fordham, *The Curse of the Great Train Robbery*, p.179.
*** Goody, *How to Rob a Train*, p.182.

Goody says that the vital inside information came from McKenna who was working at the Post Office Sorting Office in Salford and not from London at all.* But how would a postman in the main sorting office at Salford have all the knowledge necessary to instruct the robbers? Unless, of course, there were one or more other insiders too – individuals who were well connected in the right places to both the Post Office and the railways. But then why would the gang have needed Patrick McKenna at all?

But putting those general issues to one side, Goody's case against Mr McKenna is:

1.   That he was an Ulsterman (by birth anyway).
2.   That he worked for the Post Office.
3.   That he was approximately the same age as the alleged insider.

And of course, very dodgy photographic identification by Goody that would stand no chance of being accepted in a court of law. Goody is the sole witness against Mr Mckenna. Apart from the fact that Goody's character has been so marred by his dishonesty as to make his claim of truthfulness hollow:

- Goody had never been an informer, and it stretches belief to accept that this would change, for no good reason, as he reached the end of his life.
- Goody had form for 'creating a good story' about the robbery – even though entirely false.
- There is at least one better suspect.
- McKenna seems to have led a blameless life and lived within his means as a postman. He died leaving just £3,000.
- The McKenna family point to the lack of any connection between Mr McKenna and the train robbers or other members of the criminal fraternity.
- Mr McKenna's role within the Post Office would not have given him access to the necessary inside information.

---

* Goody, *How to Rob a Train*, p.182.

In fact, when the Post Office Investigation Department created a list of the hundreds of Post Office employees that would have had access to information about the TPO, McKenna's name did not even appear.

Goody says in *How to Rob a Train* that the first time he met the Ulsterman was when he was introduced to him in Finsbury Park. At this stage there was no clue to his identity:

> He was apparently a postal worker employed on the Travelling Post Office … like myself, he had been raised in Northern Ireland … he was quite a bit older than me … he had risen to the rank of senior postman and had all the information we needed as to the contents of the high value package.**

(What he meant by 'the high value package' is unknown, but it is taken verbatim from his book.)

The second meeting that allegedly took place was, according to that same book, at Marble Arch. Goody, calling the Ulsterman 'Freddie', describes how the insider tells him the job could be worth up to £5 million. The last meeting between them took place, allegedly, at Green Park in Central London. He describes a warm summer afternoon and the two of them in discussion while sitting on the grass. He says, 'Freddie got up (from the grass), "Anyone fancy an ice cream?" He asked.'

Goody then describes how Freddie (the Ulsterman) wandered off to an ice cream kiosk, leaving his jacket on the grass:

> In the exposed inside pocket I spotted a spectacle case, so I slipped it out and opened it. I was curious about the guy and it was an opportunity to find out a bit more about him. Inside was an optician's label with an address in Lisburn, Northern Ireland. The prescription was in the name of one Patrick McKenna…

** Goody, *How to Rob a Train*, p.84.

However, in the later film entitled *The Great British Train Robbery: A Tale of Two Thieves* (Signature Entertainment, 2014) Goody says the first meeting was in Kensington Gardens.

And elsewhere Goody says it was at the last meeting that took place on 31 July 1963 in Kensington Gardens that the Ulsterman got up to get a cup of tea, leaving his jacket on a chair. He says the Ulsterman's spectacle case was sticking out from the jacket pocket, and in this account he adds, 'Sewn on the inside pocket of the jacket was the name of an Ulster tailor.'[*]

As you can see, these vital accounts vary significantly in location and content. But even if the accounts given by Goody did not differ, even if they were similar enough to be plausible, you would be stretched to believe the story. We are asked to believe that a 19-year-old left Ireland wearing a jacket from a local tailor, and thirty years later he was still the same jacket size, and still wearing the thirty-year-old jacket. Does all this seem credible to you?

Goody is consistent in one important respect: he maintains that it was at the final meeting on 31 July 1963 that the vital information necessary to carry out the robbery was imparted:

> Paddy had intimate details of timetables and security. The van carrying the money, the High Value Package, was normally the second car from the engine and contained five or six postal workers. The next section of the train was a mobile sorting office with about 70 postal workers. Paddy (Freddie/Ulsterman) now reckoned that at holiday periods we could be talking in the region of £6 million.[**]

Yet, the prosecution case was based on evidence that the conspiracy to rob the train started much earlier than that. The main count on the indictment against the robbers read like this:

> On divers day unknown between the first day of May 1963 and the ninth day of August 1963 in the County of

---

[*]   Russell-Pavier/Richards, *Crime of the Century*, p.58.

[**] Goody, *How to Rob a Train*.

Buckinghamshire conspired together and with other persons unknown to stop a mail with intent to rob the said mail.

Having heard all the evidence given to the court, Fordham concluded that there was good reason to believe that the prosecution had the dates for the conspiracy set right. She heard evidence that by 1 May 1963, the TPO train running over the August Bank Holiday had been identified as the best target, Sears Crossing signals had been selected as the place to stop the train and Bridego Bridge chosen as the place at which the mails would be offloaded.[***]

Fordham's account was fully corroborated to me in person by Tom Wisbey. In addition there is other good evidence to show that the GTR was at an advanced stage of planning months before Goody alleges.

During 1962, Reynolds, Wilson, Goody, one Mickey Ball and others carried out a robbery at Heathrow that netted them £62,000. Ball was quickly arrested and in a written statement said, 'Well, you won't get me for the big job anyway.' It is surely reasonable to assume, like others, that Ball was referring to the Great Train Robbery as 'the big one'. [****]This was at least eight months before the Great Train Robbery and quite contrary to Goody's assertions.

Fordham goes further:

It can be safely assumed that all the main details were settled some months before the London airport raid. By this time, they knew the gang to be used, the train to be stopped, and the dates after a Bank Holiday … It could, I was assured, have been done by the previous Easter (Spring 1963), but the August date was selected for its fortunate coincidence of Scottish and English leisure, thus making a heavier load probable. [*****]

[***]   Fordham, *The Robbers' Tale*, p.50.
[****]   Fordham, *The Robbers' Tale*, p.34.
[*****] Fordham, *The Robbers' Tale*, p.39.

In addition, of course, we have the Irish Mail train robbery of February 1963, which really does appear to be a rehearsal. Now, either Goody is telling the truth about his knowledge of the Ulsterman, or it is fiction. We might believe Goody was making an attempt to fairly recall events that took place over fifty years ago. We might decide that it doesn't matter if he recalls 'ice cream' on one occasion and 'tea' on another, or whether the meeting took place in Kensington Park or Green Park, but even then we have to address the following.

If you were planning the robbery you would, I suggest, put events in the following order:

a)   Obtain details of the times the train was due to stop at every location en route.

b)   Choose the right location for the attack, paying attention to the need to ensure that adequate time would be afforded to seize control of the train, separate the TPO coach from the train, move the TPO coach to a suitable location and break into it, subdue the postmen, remove the mailbags and make good escape to a hideout.

c)   Choose a hideout – Leatherslade Farm.

Yet we know from evidence put before the court that Leatherslade Farm was definitely acquired by the bandits well before 31 July 1963. So it seems Goody is asking us to believe the farm was actually obtained after that date, and all other arrangements for the robbery were also made in the eight days that followed. That, of course, would have been impossible.

Alternatively, if the meeting did take place on 31 July as alleged, then the farm must have been purchased before the location of the attack had been determined. That, of course, would be ridiculous.

So, when I read Goody's nonsense, and worse, having seen it generally accepted as true, I felt the need to speak to the McKenna family. It is several years ago now, perhaps five. I traced them easily enough and spoke to Mark McKenna, grandson of the wrongly accused, Patrick. He was clearly delighted in my interest in the matter. He described how awful it had been to have his beloved grandfather dishonoured by it all.

Mark later wrote to me and explained how the identification of his grandfather (by Goody) had taken place (see Mark's letter in Appendix 1). Mark's mother has also had to live with the shame and unfair notoriety attaching to their family.

The way that the press went about naming 'Patrick McKenna' resulted in no conclusive evidence whatsoever and created unnecessary worry to an elderly widow and her family. Mark told me he was invited to a viewing of the launch of a film that 'exposed' his grandfather as one of the gang. As the film finished he felt choked and angry. One of the senior men involved in the production (he named him) patted him on the back and said something like, 'You're lucky Mark that your grandfather isn't still alive, he'd be facing jail.' Mark told me that he had trouble containing his emotions. I can well imagine it.

Remember, for Patrick McKenna, postman, to be the Ulsterman, he would have had to:

1. Advise which TPO route would be the richest (there were numerous TPO trains).
2. Advise on what time of the year would see the biggest payday (after a bank holiday weekend).
3. Provide detailed information on the layout of signals.
4. Know BR procedures for guards, drivers, signalmen and linemen in the event of a signal's failure.
5. Be in a position to advise on the night whether a full load had been dispatched from Glasgow.
6. Advise and arrange for the sabotage and removal from service of the high-security TPO coaches.

The new coaches had been fitted with added bolts to strengthened doors, metal bars fitted to the windows and not least, bandit alarms.

I can tell you from personal experience that the bandit alarms almost certainly would have prevented the crime or caused its immediate detection. Years later I heard them on several occasions, not during an attack but when they were set off accidentally or as a result of a fault. The alarms could be heard far and wide and on a still night in isolated country, literally for a mile or more. The recording went something like 'Help ... This is the Travelling Post office ... We are being attacked ... Call the police ... dial 999' and this was repeated and repeated.

But none of that was to be. Instead, by some remarkable coincidence that had never occurred before, all three special TPO coaches were out of commission. Officially, they were recorded as having the following faults:

- Hot Axle box (out of commission 4 July)
- Held at Euston – flat tyre (out of commission 1 August)
- Hot axle box (then other defects too, out of commission 23 June)

All three of those TPO coaches were supposed to have been repaired at Swindon railway engineering works, but at least two were said to have been at Willesden (North London) on the night of the robbery.

Establishing whether these coaches had been sabotaged was vital to uncovering that part of the criminal conspiracy seated within the railways. Yet little seems to have been done by the Transport Police to get beyond the superficial.

We know that a BR engineer made a formal statement that the coaches were out of service because of the mechanical faults listed. But the world seems to have let it rest there. As you have already read, British Rail were experts at covering their backs, and always tried to keep very tight control of internal matters. Put bluntly, I believe that BR would have concealed the truth in order to deflect or prevent blame to themselves.

You might be asking how difficult it would be to put a TPO carriage out of action. The answer, I know now, is simple. I have discovered that it was done more than once by criminals, especially north of the border. All they had to do was shove a scrunched-up newspaper in a coach's connecting vacuum pipes and it would then be impossible for the train to which it was connected to move forward. Was such a method used on those more secure TPO carriages in order to keep them out of service? We will never know.

Cook quotes Commander Hatherill on this point:

> According to Commander Hatherill, Mrs Wilson (wife of train robber Wilson) had confirmed that our suspicions were correct with regards to sabotage; the vans were put out of action so as to ensure that an older and less secure type of van … would be in use. [*]

So what have the robbers had to say on the issue? After all, several have been gushing about most other aspects of the robbery. They have said little indeed. But Gordon Goody admits that the robbers were fully aware of the significance of the more secure TPO coaches and the essential need to ensure they were not in use. He says that in conversation with the Ulsterman, well in advance of the attack, 'I asked McKenna about it and he said not to worry, on the night of the robbery the van would be of the older type.'[**]

We know that the highly acclaimed Detective Chief Superintendent Butler, who headed the GTR investigation of course, was opposed to the very idea of there being an insider. But no independent analysis of the facts can result in any real doubt. I think it most likely that DCS Butler would have wanted the world to believe that if there had been such an insider, he would have captured him.

So, let's start from scratch. If you were looking to identify the insider, what would be the first question you would pose? It would surely be, what sort of occupation would you hold in order to be able to glean all the information needed? You would conclude that there are only two possible answers:

---

[*]   Cook, *The Untold Story*.
[**] Goody, *How to Rob A Train*, p.91.

(a) There was not one insider but at least two. One would have to be a senior postal worker with access to information about the size of the consignment from Glasgow and the number of bags being loaded as the train made its journey south. He would have to communicate this to the waiting robbers. The other would need to be a well-placed railway employee who, apart from anything else, could get to the high-security TPO coaches and sabotage them. He would also need to be able to obtain keys for the signals (Yes, did you know they were padlocked? Keys were used to unlock them.) and know all about the likely signalman's response to the unexpected stopping of the train.

OR

(b) there was just one well-placed culprit who was in a trusted position and engaged operationally on the railways. He would need to be able to access all the information outlined in (a) above. So what sort of occupation would fit that bill? What about a highly placed Post Office worker? No. There was no member of the Post Office staff who would have had such a broad access to railway information, or technical knowledge of signals, the track layout, BR rules governing driver, guard and signalmen, or to access the TPO coaches in railway sidings or railway workshops in order to locate and sabotage them.

Remember this insider was able to warn the gang that the load was light on the night of the intended raid – the 6/7 August – and cause the robbery to be delayed by twenty-four hours. He was also able to get a final message sent on the night of the robbery, from the north of England, stipulating the size of the load.

In her book, Peta Fordham who, of course, had interviewed at least two of the robbers during or after trial, describes asking them about their reaction to the sudden twenty-four-hour postponement of the raid, says, 'The interval caused immediate anxiety lest the new coaches should be put back.'* This is a telling sentence.

---

* Fordham, *The Robbers' Tale*, p.61.

If she is recording accurately, it proves positively that the robbers knew that the high-security TPOs should have been deployed on the night of the intended attack. It clearly indicates sabotage.

So, what is left of the case against McKenna? He was an Ulsterman, by birth anyway. Secondly, he worked for the Post Office. Finally, he was allegedly approximately the same age as the insider.

These three facts, which Mr McKenna is undoubtedly guilty of, are shared by approximately 20,000 other Ulster-born former postmen. So who was the real insider?

In January 1964, only months after the GTR, New Scotland Yard received information that individuals associated with the Great Train Robbery were planning another TPO attack, this time on a Southern Region train. Commander Hatherill and other very senior police staff accepted this as genuine.

The information received was considered so true and accurate, in fact, that several police forces worked together on what they titled 'Operation Primrose'. Coordination meetings were held at Hampshire Police headquarters in Winchester; the target of the robbers: the Weymouth to Waterloo 'Up' TPO.

That crime was said to have been planned to take place in that spring of 1964. Records of police meetings were marked as 'secret'. The police response included putting BTP detectives on the train that was expected to be attacked.

The police and the Post Office were clearly playing their cards close to their chest. Nevertheless, the *Daily Express*, which had played a major part in publicising train robberies prior to the Great Train Robbery, and that case in particular, had somehow got wind of the information. Their lead reporter on this was a man called Hoskins. Cook says:

> Hoskins put his finger right away on the issue of inside information. It seems clear, as he concludes, that whoever the mysterious inside man was at the Post Office, he had to be a particularly high-ranking official. The day after the Daily Express broke the story, post office security officials got together to discuss strategy now that the story was public ...

It seems clear that they and their colleagues were much more interested in trying to discover who leaked the ... story to the press than who leaked the inside information about the South West TPO train to a criminal gang bent on robbing it.*

It is clear that the gang behind the train robberies had a well-positioned insider. But who was it?

Gordon Goody and his accomplices have described how, prior to the GTR, they planned attacks on trains on the Weymouth to Waterloo line. They have also described vividly their plan to attack the gold train that moved bullion from Southampton Docks to Waterloo. Goody says that Buster Edwards bought a porter at Waterloo a 'gargle' (drink) and that the porter gave him all the necessary information about the gold train. Goody alleges that following receipt of that information, he and his team went to Southampton Docks and watched the gold being removed from the Union Castle Line ship and loaded onto the special train.**

Well, one thing is certain. I saw much more of those bullion movements than Mr Goody ever did. I served at Southampton Docks and witnessed the process many times. That's not important in itself, but what I can definitely say is that security was too tight for Goody and gang to observe what he claims to have seen. His claims are false.

Basically, the ship would be berthed right next to the adjacent 'shed' (in fact a huge warehouse). A dock crane would haul small wooden boxes of gold from the hold of the ship and place them close to the shed doors. The boxes would be moved straight across the shed floor and onto the special train, which was waiting inside the enclosed shed.

The security arrangements permitted no one to be within the docks unless on business, and every entrance to the docks was policed. This created what today we would call 'an outer security cordon'. This was fairly 'leaky', but at the Union

---

* Cook, *The Untold Story*.
** Goody, *How to Rob a Train*, pp.79–79.

Castle berth itself, a more thorough cordon was put in place. Barriers were erected to prevent any unauthorised entry to the shed or adjacent dockside. These barriers were policed. They were not 'leaky'.

The final cordon was inside the relevant shed. Only police officers, officials, a small number of essential dock workers and the train crew were permitted. My colleagues, and sometimes I, some of us visibly armed, observed closely. This was a 'hygienic' operation. Once it was loaded, two of my colleagues would accompany the gold as it travelled non-stop to Waterloo where a similarly strong reception party awaited.

My point is that the robbers had accurate, highly confidential security information about:

a)   Gold bullion movements from Southampton Docks
b)   TPOs travelling on the BR Southern Region
c)   TPOs travelling on BR London Midland Region

That information could not have come from the Post Office or one source working on any single BR region, or indeed the railway industry alone (it clearly involved both docks and railways). Therefore, if there were a single source, then that source must have been positioned in a senior 'security' role within an organisation responsible for both the entire rail network and the docks. There was only one organisation that fits and, I hesitate to say it, but it is the British Transport Police. I believe the true insider, the main insider, may have been a corrupt Transport CID officer.

Up to the 1980s, British Transport Police (formerly British Transport Commission Police) had responsibility (inter alia) for policing the railways and many of the country's major ports including Southampton. Most of the thousands of BTP officers then serving would have spent most of their careers based either in the docks or on the railways. Most would have spent all of their years stationed in one industry only and within that industry, in one area of the country only. The vast majority would therefore have known little of other parts of the country or the other nationalised transport industry in which they did not work.

But at Force Headquarters, a group of officers had national responsibility and could and would travel across the entire BR and Docks network, visiting Southampton Docks and other ports. They had unrestricted access and would never be challenged. That group was BTP headquarters CID. They spent a great deal of their time investigating serious crime including theft of mail-bags, and had close liaison with the Post Office Investigation Department and the secrets they carried.

Believe me, the Headquarters CID staff were no 'boy scouts'. They were typical of the detectives of the time. Many of them were Londoners and had developed relationships with London-based railway thieves. Bearing all that in mind, certain unresolved issues could begin to make sense.

For instance, we know the BTP headquarters CID were tasked with finding the corrupt insider. We know it is reported that they spent a great deal of time and effort diligently trying to do that. Their abject failure would be understandable if a corrupt member of their team were in a position to stay one step ahead of their investigations.

We know that Scotland Yard and the Buckinghamshire Constabulary put their absolute best efforts into retrieving any forensic evidence available from the railway crime scene. It was a widespread area encompassing the two coaches, the signals that had been interfered with, the engine of the train, the emergency signal phones, and areas of criminal activity around Bridego Bridge. All of these, every constable should have known, needed to be preserved for detailed examination by fingerprint officers, scenes-of-crime staff or scientific specialists.

The earliest senior detective officer at the scene was, it seems, Detective Superintendent Ward of the Transport Police. From examination of the statements given by rail staff to the British Railways internal enquiry, it seems that Mr Ward was on the scene by about 6 a.m., perhaps as late as late as 6.30. I believe he lived at Ruislip at the time.

We know that the Railway Control Centre at Euston reported the crime to the BTP and NSY at 4.20 a.m. If the BTP Control Room phoned Mr Ward immediately and he roused himself quickly, he would then have had a 20-mile journey (pre M25) to complete. He was obviously quickly off the mark.

Evidence heard at the BR enquiry shows that a BR signal engineer, with Mr Ward present, worked on the signals that had been altered by the bandits, before any specialist forensic work was done. That should not have happened. The evidence also shows that Detective Superintendent Ward took possession of pieces of wire from the signal engineer. The robbers seem to have added these wires to, or cut them from, the signalling equipment.

In addition, the evidence shows that the engineer recovered a discarded signal padlock that had been unlocked and removed from the signals by the robbers (by the use of a key). The padlock was found by the tracks near the signals. But where is that potentially important BR Internal Enquiry evidence ever referred to again? The last we see it referred to is when Mr Ward takes possession.

What has been known since 8 August 1963 is that the locomotive on which Driver Mills was assaulted, where a struggle involving several robbers had taken place, where much fingerprint and other evidence might have been found, was, incredibly, hurriedly removed from the scene. It was dispatched to Crewe where it remained for thirty-six hours.

None of this might have been Mr Ward's fault, and I know nothing to his detriment – I did not know him. I have no reason to have any doubts about his character. He seems to have been well regarded by everyone and a few years later he was promoted further. Perhaps he made a full report about all of these things. It might have been filed away somewhere and long since lost. All that remains now are the anomalies, and they give rise to unanswered questions.

I do know very well that some senior officers would sometimes respond to 'front-page events' unpredictably. I first became aware of that as a young CID aide. I was based at Southampton Docks when a big cruise ship was set on fire during the night whilst in port. It was a substantial blaze. I'm sorry to say I can't remember the name of the vessel now, but it might have been SS *Canberra*.

Anyway, the ship's crew immediately suspected arson and, along with the fire service, police were called. The BTP's leader at Southampton was a kindly man. He was phoned immediately and rushed down to the scene to take command – in his pyjamas and slippers.

That's a true story. If he had taken time to reflect before rushing from his bed, he might have thought better of it. But that's the way it goes when stuff hits the fan at three in the morning.

We know the train robbers took six pairs of handcuffs with them. We also know that Goody refers to them in his autobiography.[*]

We know that both Driver Mills and his second man were left handcuffed together at the scene of the robbery. When the local police attended the scene and tried to free them they found the handcuffs were 'American style' and they had no key to fit. Clearly, the 'cuffs were not standard police issue. However, long ago, another transport policeman, in hushed tones, told me confidentially that 'Hyatt', an American company, had manufactured the handcuffs used. That officer also told me that at the time of the robbery only two police forces in the UK were using that type of handcuffs: the Transport Police and the Metropolitan.

The Transport Police used them more freely. Every constable had a set on a personal issue basis, and if lost, replacements were issued. However, the Met only allowed them to be booked out from the police station against a signature, and after every use they had to be returned to the station and signed back in. Some reports indicate the handcuffs used on Driver Mills and his Second Man were cut from their wrists by the local fire brigade, but other records indicate that at about 5.30 a.m. on the day of the attack, a senior Met officer was able to supply a key.

When the police searched Leatherslade Farm, they found amongst the many items left behind by the robbers printed

---

[*] Goody, *How to Rob a Train*, location 1159.

instructions for the use of the handcuffs. As Russell-Pavier/
Richards point out:

> The handcuffs used by the gang were unusual, being American
> and the very latest design. This detail offered another poten-
> tially useful clue, yet there is no mention in the early stages
> of the investigation of detectives trying to trace the origin of
> the cuffs. **

But nowhere is it possible to find any reference to the name of
the handcuff manufacturer.

When police enquiries were later carried out as to the origin
of the handcuffs, it seems that a Birmingham company was identified, but not named, as the likely supplier. They were apparently
contacted by the police and claimed to have a full record of all
sales. Yet that line of enquiry seems to have come to an abrupt
stop. Nothing more is said on the subject.

Working on the basis that I believed the information I was
given years ago was true, I first looked to see if the Hyatt company had any connection to Birmingham. My research quickly
showed that Hyatt has no more to do with Birmingham than
Elvis does to Graceland. The Hyatt company was formed in
Birmingham 200 years ago and much later forged a Trans-
Atlantic company.

I still had not confirmed that the handcuffs used on Driver
Mills were made by Hyatt, so I approached the helpful staff at
the Metropolitan Police's crime museum knowing that they held
GTR exhibits. I asked if they had the handcuff exhibits or photographs of them. They told me they had neither but suggested I
contact the Thames Valley Police Museum. This I did.

I spoke to another very helpful individual, PC Colin Boyes.
He explained to me that the museum had for many years displayed 'the handcuffs used to restrain Driver Mills and Second
Man Whitby' (see overleaf). Naturally, I asked him the name of
the handcuff manufacturer and he responded, 'Bean Cobb'. I

** Russell-Pavier/Richards, *Crime of the Century*, p.71.

was surprised, disappointed even. I told him about my suspicion. Then he told me a revealing story.

In 2015, more than fifty years after the event, an elderly retired fireman from the local fire brigade, William Perry, visited him. He wanted to donate a link from a pair of handcuffs. Mr Perry said that on the morning of the Great Train Robbery he had been called to the local hospital, the Royal Buckinghamshire. There he was taken to see two patients, Mills and Whitby, who were handcuffed together. Using bolt-croppers he severed the handcuff links. He kept the severed link (see overleaf) as a token and put it in his wife's jewellery box where it had remained ever since.

But links on their own would not prove the cuffs to be Hyatt without forensic science work and I haven't been able to access that for many years. Further research revealed a former DC John Bailey and his scrapbooks. He had been part of the Great Train Robbery investigation from day one. Furthermore, he had been involved in the photographic and fingerprint evidence

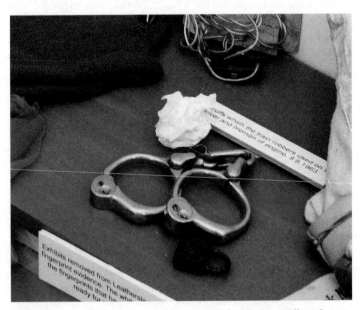

Handcuffs wrongly displayed as being those used on Driver Mills and Second Man Whitby.

gathering and had kept a huge collection of photographs. Thanks to Bournemouth Newspapers I was able to view a photo of the handcuffs that were truly used to secure Mills and Whitby.

You can clearly see on the photograph (see overleaf) that at some stage after the cuffs had been severed by bolt croppers (by that fireman), they have been held with string (for the purpose of display).

I have compared the shape, finish and mechanism of the handcuffs photographed by DC John Bailey with those handcuffs issued to me on a personal basis, and which were close by my side for over thirty years. I can tell you without doubt that the cuffs DC John Bailey photographed during the early days of the Great Train Robbery, and which the train robbers used on Driver Mills and his Second Man, were Hyatt.

I have been told recently by a former BTP CID colleague serving at the time of the GTR, that shortly after the Great Train Robbery he and all of his colleagues had to produce for

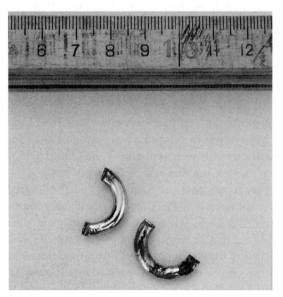

The link cut from the Hyatt handcuffs by the Fire Service at the hospital when Mills and Whitby were receiving treatment immediately after the robbery.

Photo of Hyatt handcuffs used to secure Driver Mills and his Second Man Whitby. Taken on 8 August 1963 by police.

inspection their Hyatt-issue handcuffs. Obviously, someone in authority thought that just maybe...

You might well ask why the Thames Valley Police Museum would have misled the public and researchers by displaying the wrong handcuffs. PC Boyce explained to me that it seems to be a simple labelling error. The handcuffs wrongly displayed he believes now to be the ones that were used on the defendants, Cordrey and Boal, to bring them to the police station after arrest. It was all a simple mistake.

So where are the 'real' handcuffs now? Well, the Thames Valley Police Museum is in temporary accommodation and many exhibits are in storage. It will take some considerable time to complete a search, but they will be there.

It is easy to see that the handcuffs, and the limited police enquiries conducted in 1963, are potentially an important lead to the truth. We know, whoever the insider was, and wherever he was employed, that he was in a position to assure the robbers that on the night of the attack the new TPOs would not be in use.

Some people have recently suggested that it must have been a high-ranking Post Office Investigation Department member. But such a person would not have the breadth of knowledge and access (signals, track layout, able to take high security TPOs out of use, etc.), but members of BTP headquarters CID were almost uniquely able to travel across the country to any part of the railway estate and inspect whatever they wished without invitation or witness.

Are there any proven links between any of the raiders and the Transport Police? Well, Cook refers to Cordrey and Welch being questioned but released in the three-year period before the GTR.[*] It is most likely that any such questioning would have been by the Transport Police. Uncharacteristically, Cook does not provide further information on the source of that information.

As stated earlier, the Gentry (1981) case would have been a very significant case for any police force or police department in the country, including the Flying Squad. So there weren't many members of the BTP, especially senior ranks, who didn't know about it. It was no surprise therefore when, about a year after the (1982) trial, an old uniform superintendent called Bob McNally sat me down in his office and asked me about it.

It was informal, and we drank tea and ate biscuits like trusted friends. Then he leaned forward as if he was concerned we might be overheard: 'The Great Train Robbery. You know we had an insider don't you Graham?' Of course, I asked him what he was talking about and how he came to know. He told me a certain senior detective had told him that he had been working 'undercover' with the villains at the time of the Great Train Robbery. I must stress it was not Superintendent Ward that was named, nor any Transport police officer mentioned elsewhere in this book.

The detective that Bob McNally named was well known to me as a scoundrel and a reputed thief. It was commonly thought they he was, or had been, in league with villains in London and involved in the thefts they committed. But I suspect that old Bob knew nothing about all that.

There was no doubting Bob McNally's sincerity; I have no doubt that the detective he named had indeed given him the account described. But why? If I had to describe the personality of the detective in question I think I would say he was a bit like

---

[*] Cook, *The Untold Story*, footnote 16 to location 373.

Bill Gentry – tough, unscrupulous, determined, single-minded, serious, violent, devious and dishonest.

So why would he tell Bob McNally such a fairy story? I have only ever been able to think of one plausible explanation. Old Bob stumbled into some evidence, or witnessed an event, that tied this bent cop to the train robbers, and the only justification for the evidence or incident that the bent cop could come up with was, 'I was/am on a secret undercover job.'

There will be many Transport Police officers from my era who remember me as ambitious and arrogant. They will also remember that I was not someone who ever 'went for a pint', I didn't 'crave peer recognition', or kowtow to senior officers. They will probably remember I was the dirtiest and most aggressive footballer they encountered too. So I wasn't (am not) the most pleasant man they ever met. BUT, they will also remember that I took on perceived police corruption without hesitation. I tell you that now because it is relevant.

Over the years, one or two of my colleagues, who will always remain unnamed, trusted me enough to tell me what they knew, or what they suspected, and kept secret about the Great Train Robbery. The Hyatt handcuffs issue is an example. Here is another. This officer named below was happy to be identified.

When I served at Southampton docks I got to know a constable called Stan Wade. Stan was in his thirties, a quiet, serious, reflective man. It will be no surprise if I tell you every day we were faced with different foreign languages. Sometimes it was just American English; most of us could cope with some of that without feeling too queasy. But on other occasions it was impossible to communicate effectively unless you spoke Italian, Greek, Gujarati, Spanish or whatever. The result was that we all soon began to make a mental note of the language skills we held between us. Stan was a fluent speaker and writer of Arabic. I mention that now as an indication of his intelligence. He had learned it during his army days.

After I published a memoir a few years ago, I received a letter from Stan. It was the first time I had heard from him in over thirty years. He said some kind words about the memoir that brought a smile to my face and then went on to describe how after we parted company in 1972 he had been posted to Glasgow where he served as a sergeant. But it was his final paragraphs that gave me a shiver. And remember, on no occasion had I ever voiced my suspicion publicly, or privately to Stan, or any other BTP officer, serving or retired, that a BTP officer might be implicated in the Great Train Robbery.

This is what Stan wrote: 'I could go on but am still of the mind that the Great Train Robbery was thought of by our CID officers in Glasgow…'

As you can imagine, I couldn't wait to hear why Stan had come to this conclusion. I visited him a few days later. He had no direct proof. But he told me he had seen real dishonesty in detectives who had served during the time of the GTR and who remained there after he arrived. He described the rumours that encircled those individuals, and the proof of dishonesty that eventually led to some of them leaving the job.

I remembered my own unhappy experiences of BTP Glasgow and my young Scottish informant who had been murdered in London by Glasgow gangsters. I do not believe that the BTP CID in Glasgow 'thought of' the Great Train Robbery, but I do know that the gangsters of Glasgow and London were in cahoots in those days whenever it was of mutual benefit. I know that there were corrupt BTP detectives in London and Glasgow at the time and they could easily have been in cahoots too.

Stan named names and told me several stories of the criminality that he was sure was taking place whilst he served in Scotland. He told me his attempts to get something done about it had created a difficult position for him with his bosses. Then he told me something more. He told me about the cases in Scotland where those wanting to stop a train moving had simply stuffed newspapers into the 'pipe that needs a vacuum' for the train to be moved. He said it was very easy to get a coach taken out of service in this way. I remembered the TPO coaches all being out of service on the night of the robbery, and suddenly I knew how easy it would have been.

Of course, back in 1963 the railways had recorded the apparent reasons these coaches had been removed from service, 'hot axle box' being one. I am not an engineer; in fact I have difficulty inflating a car tyre. But it is clear now that getting a TPO coach taken out of service would not be difficult if you could get access.

What did Tom Wisbey say on the subject of a crooked BTP man being involved? Well, he didn't want to talk about it at all. He was never a police informer. But after several meetings and my repeated suspicions, he just nodded, 'Alright'. Did he give me any proof? No. Did he give me a name? No. Did he swear by the Almighty that a bent Transport Police detective was involved? No, nothing like. Did I feel that he had given me a positive indication? Yes, but that is all it was.

One question I haven't addressed at all so far is the name itself: The Ulsterman. Was there ever a person known by that name? Well, Tommy Wisbey when he was a member of the South Coast Raiders was still enjoying the company of a childhood friend called Lenny Holstermann. (Not his real name. During the course of writing this book I was told that the family concerned did not want their real name published. I have therefore slightly changed both first name and family name, though they remain phonetically similar.)

One of Tom's first jobs after leaving school was to work in Lenny's father's bottling factory. Tom told me that by the late 1950s, Lenny was a successful and rather 'flash' bookmaker. But, like most bookies of the time, he 'did a bit on the side' as well. Sometimes the bit on the side was supplying items for Tom's illicit use; sometimes it was getting rid (selling) items that Tom wanted quietly sold.

I wasn't ever quite sure if Lenny was regularly known to some people as 'The Ulsterman' simply because of the useful similarity in sound and added security that a false name would afford. But Tom did say that confusion had been caused amongst the gang by a mishearing of his name.

After Tom's death I mentioned this to Marilyn Wisbey. She knew exactly who I was talking about. She spoke warmly of the man who visited their home regularly throughout Tom's long period of imprisonment. She told me it was Lenny who always made sure that Marilyn and her family had food on the table and at least one holiday a year. She remembered him with great affection, as did Tom.

Marilyn told me that Lenny's wife is still alive, and she contacted her for me. At first, she was enthusiastic to get involved and to talk to me, but after a couple of days, before I had chance to meet with her, she changed her mind. I didn't trouble her again. But one thing she did say was that after the Great Train Robbery her husband had a visit from the police. Apparently, they were suspicious, but nothing came of it.

Within a couple of years of the Great Train Robbery, the Holstermanns moved from south London to a much more pleasant, though more expensive, place a few miles out. I have no proof of their involvement in anything unlawful.

POSTSCRIPT

This book will not end the speculation about the Great Train Robbery. I am aware that I might have settled one or two questions but raised further ones. However, I do think this publication takes us a step further to arriving at the full truth and rights an injustice regarding Patrick McKenna in the process.

I have in the preceding pages mentioned the novel that Tom Wisbey contributed to (*South Coast Raiders*). It mixes fact and fiction to bring to life the facts revealed in this book. It starts with the successful exploits of the South Raiders in about 1961 and follows the progress of his gang as their infamy grows.

It introduces the bent railway detective, notionally called Aldridge, and describes how he provides vital inside information to Billy Hill who, following information from Aldridge, is planning the Great Train Robbery. Under Hill's orders, Aldridge entraps the gang into working with the Krays and participating in the Great Train Robbery, something they had been loath to do.

At a late stage in the proceedings, Aldridge belatedly finds out that the Raiders have taken on an additional gang member, Alfredo (fictitious). Aldridge is forced to tell Hill, who is furious.

Young Alfredo is recently married and when his wife (Shirley) finds out that the TPO robbery is planned and that her husband is mixing with the Krays, she concludes it will end in disaster. She becomes determined to ensure that her husband has nothing to do with it.

In desperation, Shirley secretly contacts the railway police CID and speaks to a new member of the mailbag investigation squad, DC Walcott. Walcott has just transferred to London from Birmingham and has not yet been seduced into corruption.

Walcott learns that some of his new colleagues are bent and conducts a discreet investigation into the confidential information that Shirley is obtaining from her husband. However, Aldridge becomes aware of Walcott's secrets and is forced to take drastic action to protect himself from the wrath of Billy Hill and from his own criminal liability.

The novel *South Coast Raiders* will be published in 2020.

APPENDIX 1

FROM MARK MCKENNA:

To answer your questions

To set the scene, my mother (Patrick's Daughter) was contacted by a lady called Ariel Bruce, she informed my mum that she had been employed to find Patrick McKenna and asked if we could provide her with some details and maybe a photo or two. There was no mention of the Great Train Robbery.

She was very vague with the details of who had employed her simply saying it was for a gentleman who had known him in the '60s and wanted to know what happened to him as they had lost touch.

We thought nothing of this and gave her the information she asked for and then didn't hear anything from her for over 6 months, at which time I received an email from her asking if she could come and meet us to discuss her finding. We arranged to meet her at a local coffee shop near where my mum lives.

She arrived accompanied by Simon Howley who was one of the producers of the documentary. She then explained why she had been search[ing] for my grandfather. She told us that 'Gordon' had given her some details and with those she tracked my grandfather down and that he was the only person who fitted all of the things 'Gordon' had said:

The five things were:

- The guy would have been around 10 years older than Gordon in the 60's (Which would make him around 40, my granddad was 42)
- His name was Patrick McKenna (It was)
- He was from Ireland (He was)
- He worked for the Post Office (He did)
- He looked like Frank Skinner (Can't see it myself)

She then explained who Gordon Goody was and that the reason they were looking for my granddad was that Gordon was set to reveal one of the last mysteries of the Great Train Robbery which was who the Ulsterman was which she said was my granddad.

We were all shocked at this and didn't really say much, they told us about the Documentary 'A Tale of two Thieves' that would be coming out and said that the newspapers/media would no doubt be in contact with us (through Simon).

As the days passed my mother became more upset over this revelation and was adamant that he[r] father would not have done this. I took it on myself to protect my mother from the media and did an interview with the Daily Mirror stating we did not believe that he had done it and I also travelled to London to see the documentary when it premiered.

I have since been researching the Robbery and have more questions now regarding who the Ulsterman is and am more and more sure that my granddad is not him.

To answer the rest if your questions:

I am married with 2 sons

My mum lives in the house that my grandfather did (he lived there from around 1980) the house he lived in before that is no longer there.

APPENDIX 2

To whom it might concern

Re. Tom Wisbey creating crime fiction with Graham Satchwell

Graham Satchwell says:

I have asked Tom Wisbey to contribute to the creation of crime fiction. I can't think of a better way to ensure that the writing is realistic and well-informed. We are thus creating fiction around crimes that actually occurred, or might have.

Tom Wisbey says:

I want to make it clear from the start that parts of the stories I am sharing with Graham Satchwell are fiction. Of course some parts of the stories might be true, and some parts might be an exaggeration, but other aspects are completely false.

I want to make it absolutely plain that I am not confessing to anything illegal or implicating anyone else in relation to any involvement that has not already been answered before the courts. However, Graham and I have agreed that in order to give the writing impact and for the purpose of creating realistic storytelling, he or I might pretend that some things are true when they are not.

Signed   Tom Wisbey...

Signed   Graham Satchwell ....

July, 2015

SELECTED BIBLIOGRAPHY

Cook, Andrew, *The Great Train Robbery: The Untold Story from the Closed Investigation Files* (2013, The History Press)

Fiennes, Gerard, *Fiennes on Rails: Fifty Years of Railways As Seen by Gerald Fiennes* (1987, David & Charles)

Fordham, Jon, *The Curse of the Great Train Robbery* (2016, Arena Books Ltd)

Fordham, Peta, *The Robbers' Tale: The Real Story of the Great Train Robbery* (1965, Hodder & Stoughton)

Goody, Gordon, *How to Rob a Train: The Man Behind Britain's Most Notorious Robbery, Among Other Things* (2014, Milo Books Limited)

Gosling, John and Craig, Dennis, *The Great Train Robbery: The Inside Story* (1964, WH Allen)

Hill, Billy, *Boss of Britain's Underworld* (2008, Billy Hill Family Limited, Kindle edition)

Morris, Jim, *The Great Train Robbery: The Three Who Escaped Justice, A Question of Alibis* (2013, www.EBookPartnership.com)

Owen, Arwel, *The Forgotten Train Robbery* (2013, Kindle eBook)

Pearson, John, *Profession of Violence: The Rise and Fall of the Kray Twins* (2015, William Collins)

Reynolds, Bruce, *The Autobiography of a Thief: The Man Behind the Great Train Robbery* (1995, Bantam Press)

Russell-Pavier, Nick and Richards, Stewart, *The Great Train Robbery: Crime of the Century: The Definitive Account* (2013, Orion Publishing Group)

Wisbey, Tommy, *Wrong Side of the Tracks: The Life Story of Great Train Robber Tommy Wisbey* (2014, Bridge Publishing)

INDEX